A Proven 7-Step Guide to
True Financial Freedom

YOUR MONEY MAP

A PROVEN 7-STEP GUIDE TO
TRUE FINANCIAL FREEDOM

HOWARD DAYTON

MOODY PUBLISHERS

CHICAGO

The name Crown Money Map™ is a trademark of Crown Financial Ministries.
Most of chapters 14 and 17 originally appeared in Howard Dayton, *Free and Clear* (Chicago: Moody, 2006), 96–98, 100–101, 116–19, 121, 133, 137–46,158–61, 168–69. Portions of chapters 11, 12, 13, 20, 21 are taken from Howard Dayton, *Free and Clear* (Chicago: Moody, 2006).

All Scripture quotations, unless otherwise indicated, are taken from the *Holy Bible, New International Version.*® NIV.® Copyright © 1973, 1978, 1984 by International Bible Society. Used by permission of Zondervan Publishing House. All rights reserved.

Scripture quotations marked NASB are taken from the *New American Standard Bible*®, Copyright © 1960, 1962, 1963, 1968, 1971, 1972, 1973, 1975, 1977, 1995 by The Lockman Foundation. Used by permission. (www.Lockman.org)

Scripture quotations marked TLB are taken from *The Living Bible* copyright © 1971. Used by permission of Tyndale House Publishers, Inc., Wheaton, Illinois 60189. All rights reserved.

Scripture quotations marked NLT are taken from the *Holy Bible, New Living Translation,* copyright © 1996. Used by permission of Tyndale House Publishers, Inc., Wheaton, Illinois 60189. All rights reserved.

Scripture quotations marked AMP are taken from *The Amplified Bible.* Copyright © 1965, 1987 by The Zondervan Corporation. *The Amplified New Testament* copyright © 1958, 1987 by The Lockman Foundation. Used by permission.

Cover Design: The DesignWorks Group, Inc.

Library of Congress Cataloging-in-Publication Data

Dayton, Howard Lape, 1943-
   Your money map : a proven 7-step guide to true financial freedom
   / by Howard Dayton.
      p. cm.
   Includes bibliographical references.
   ISBN-13: 978-0-8024-6869-7
   1. Finance, Personal–Religious aspects–Christianity. 2. Finance,
Personal–Biblical teaching.   I. Title.
HG179.D373 2007
332.024'01–dc22

2006029582

ISBN: 0-8024-6869-1
ISBN-13: 978-0-8024-6869-7

We hope you enjoy this book from Moody Publishers. Our goal is to provide high-quality, thought-provoking books and products that connect truth to your real needs and challenges. For more information on other books and products written and produced from a biblical perspective, go to www.moodypublishers.com or write to:

Moody Publishers
820 N. LaSalle Boulevard
Chicago, IL 60610

1 3 5 7 9 10 8 6 4 2

Printed in the United States of America

To Bev Dayton,
my wife of more than thirty years and my closest friend.
I am incredibly grateful we made the journey
to True Financial Freedom together.

Matthew and Danielle,
who have been a relentless joy as children and now as adults.
And to Michelle and Kyle;
I am so thankful you are a part of our family.

To Chuck Bentley,
for creating the Crown Money Map
and his vision to use it to help so many people.

Finally, to The Crown Financial Ministries family.
You mean more to me than I can ever say.

CONTENTS

ACKNOWLEDGMENTS

I am grateful to several key people who have shaped my life: Ken Connor, Jess Correll, George Fooshee, Tim Manor, Lyston Peebles, Jim Seneff, Stan Walker, and John White. My thanks also to Dave Rae, Stan Reiff, Andres Panasiuk, and Sharon Epps—all remarkable leaders.

Finally, a special thanks to Jack Alexander, Ron Blue, Steady Cash, Tom Darden, Daryl Heald, Bill Leonard, Scott Melby, Terry Parker, Jim Shoemaker, Andy Stanley— for your generous gifts of time, resources and guidance.

GETTING THE
MOST
FROM THIS BOOK

This book will transform your life and your finances, because you will be learning what the God of the universe says about handling money. *Your Money Map* is for everyone—single or married, young or old, whether you earn a lot or a little.

Regardless of your present financial situation, I urge you to read through the entire book to understand the big picture of what God wants you to know about handling money. You'll learn about seven destinations on the road to true financial freedom. Once you discover where you are on the journey, carefully read the chapters addressing *your* next destination. When you arrive there, review the chapters that will help you reach the following destination.

Your Money Map is designed for you to interact with. Don't just *read* this book. Personalize it. Underline it. Write notes in it. Make it *yours* as you complete your financial information. Review and update your progress. The books that have helped me the most are the ones that I interacted with, not just quickly read.

If you are married, study this book with your spouse. If you are single, do it with a friend. Better yet, become part of a small group to encourage one another to apply what you are learning.

Your Money Map includes four features to assist you on your journey to true financial freedom:

1. *Discussion questions.* The book is divided into six sections and at the end of each section are discussion questions. Meet with your friend or group to answer the questions, discuss what you read, and bounce ideas off each other. This will help you enormously.

2. *Tools for the journey.* At the end of each section, we list some outstanding books, Web sites, financial tools, and organizations that will help you on your journey to true financial freedom.

3. *Roadside Assistance—Online!* At the end of most chapters you will find *Roadside Assistance—Online!* which identifies some of the *free* online tools, forms, information, and assistance that you can access at CrownMoneyMap.org.

4. *CrownMoneyMap.org.* CrownMoneyMap.org is a dynamic Web site created to accompany this book. It contains special online tools, videos, and answers to frequently asked questions. On it you will be able to create your personalized journey to true financial freedom, track your progress, and store and modify information—and share it with others in the Money Map community! Join us and be encouraged.

As I wrote this book, I often prayed that you would experience the awesome sense of hope, peace, and confidence that comes from discovering God's way of handling money. I am excited because I know great things are going to happen to you. They happened to me, and I have never been the same.

So let's get started together.

PART

1

PREPARE *for the* JOURNEY

If a person gets his attitude toward money straight, it will straighten out almost every other area of his life.

— BILLY GRAHAM

THE CHALLENGE

It was finally time. My wife, Bev, and I had decided years ago to drive our car until the wheels were ready to fall off. After 185,000 miles, it was time to trade in the "blue bomber."

We drove to a dealership that had a good reputation for selling low-mileage used cars. As we pulled up, a salesman approached us. "Hi. Name is Matt Mitchell. Can I help you?"

Matt was young and likeable, with a smile that lit up his face. We chose a car, agreed on a price, and he invited us into his office.

"Let's fill out the paperwork and the car will be yours," he said, reaching into his desk for a stack of forms. After we completed them he said, "Next stop is the finance department. You've got to pay for this beauty, you know."

"Oh, we don't need to meet with the finance department. We'll just pay cash for it," Bev said. "We've been saving for this for several years."

"What? You've got to be kidding!" Matt responded with a look of disbelief. "I'm really curious. How'd you do it?"

"A number of years ago we learned what God says about money, and it completely changed how we handle our finances," I responded.

"God says something about money?" Matt interrupted. "He says something about saving up to buy a car for cash?"

"Well," I chuckled, "He didn't mention anything about buying cars, but the Bible contains 2,350 verses on how to handle money and possessions. You might be surprised to learn that 15 percent of everything Jesus Christ said had to do with it. In fact, He talked more about money than almost any other subject. He knew money would be a challenge for all of us, and He cared enough to show us how to handle it wisely."

The expression on Matt's face changed from skepticism to sincere interest. "Look, I wonder if my wife and I could talk with you. We're, well, we're in real financial trouble," he stammered. "Not to mention that Jennifer is expecting our second child in about three months.

"And most of our friends are also struggling financially. It doesn't seem to matter their age, or if they're single or married—or even how much they earn. Some of them are making good money, too. They all have too much debt and not enough savings. Job security doesn't seem to exist anymore, and I don't know many seriously planning for retirement.

"On top of everything else, Jennifer and I have a gnawing feeling there are serious problems in our country's economy—problems that could affect us someday. We don't know what to do next. We don't know where to turn for help. Frankly, we're a little scared."

STARTLING STATS:

America is now absorbing about 80 percent of the entire world's surplus savings to fund its deficits and debts. This can't continue forever.[1]

"Matt, you're right to be concerned," I said. "There are huge problems facing our economy. Global competition from emerging powerhouses like China and India, losing jobs to outsourcing overseas, a Social Security system that is projected to run out of money, the skyrocketing cost of health care and gasoline, the threat of terrorism, and mind-boggling federal debt and trade deficits—well, the list just goes on and on.

"Hey . . . here's an idea. Bev and I could meet with you and Jennifer and talk about your finances," I said. "We'd love to get together. Give me your address, and I'll send you a form to complete that will help us better understand your situation. It's called a financial statement, and on it you'll list everything you own and everything you owe."

Matt agreed.

As we drove home, Bev said what I had been thinking about during our first meeting with the Mitchells. "Don't forget to send that financial statement you promised Matt. I really want to meet Jennifer and help them get turned around."

Roadside Assistance—Online!

Do you believe there are 2,350 verses in the Bible dealing with money and possessions? Visit **CrownMoneyMap.org** for the complete list of them arranged by topics. Remember, it is free.

*How we handle money is simply an outside indicator
of our internal spiritual condition.*

—LARRY BURKETT

Cofounder of Crown Financial Ministries

THE
SOLUTION

A week later, Bev and I met with Matt and Jennifer.

"How did the two of you first meet?" Bev asked.

"Well, I met Matt just the way you did," Jennifer replied. "I needed to buy a car, and Matt was the salesman. After we'd spent just a few minutes together, I knew he was something special."

"And I felt the same way," Matt chimed in, smiling. "It was amazing—two people so different from each other falling in love.

"I'm a salesman; Jennifer teaches the fourth grade. I always look at the big picture; Jennifer is great with details. And . . . " he added sheepishly, "I'm a spender; she's a saver."

"Some of our differences are because of our family backgrounds," Jennifer explained. "After my parents divorced, I was raised by my mom, and we had to watch every penny. Matt's parents spent whatever they wanted, but money became a huge source of conflict between them. They ended up fighting about it a lot."

"That's right," Matt acknowledged. "And when Jennifer and I were filling out the financial statement you gave us, we ended up in an argument."

I saw color creeping into Jennifer's face as she added, "It was bad news. We had no idea how much trouble we were in. The reality of owing a lot more than we owned triggered a lot of emotion, and we didn't handle it well."

"But the good news is that you now know the facts," I responded. "The Bible says, *'Any enterprise is built by wise planning, becomes strong through common sense, and profits wonderfully by **keeping abreast of the facts.**'*[1] It's nearly impossible to make wise financial decisions without facing the facts."

BEEN THERE—DONE THAT

When the Mitchells shared their situation, I understood how they felt. Before learning God's way of handling money, Bev and I had been on the hook for a ton of debt and had little savings.

However, once we learned and applied God's financial principles, *everything* changed. And I mean everything! It didn't happen overnight, but within ten years we were financially free. We were completely debt-free— including our home—had savings in the bank, and had become much more generous. We had come from financial bondage to financial freedom. Words cannot describe how good it felt. Now I want you to experience this same freedom.

Someone once told me that God often allows a person to teach a subject because the *teacher* desperately needs it! That is true for me. I have never met anyone who had more wrong attitudes about money or who handled it more contrary to the Bible than I did.

STARTLING STATS:

Two of every three middle-income Americans—66 percent—live from paycheck to paycheck.

Some of you reading this book are in deep financial difficulty. You may feel as if you are suffocating under a load of bills and debts. Others of you fear you can't make fast enough progress with your finances. But with God's help you *can* make real progress. Crown Financial Ministries has worked with literally millions of people. I know from experience there is *hope* for you. I have repeatedly seen God bless the efforts of those who apply His financial principles. The Bible says, *"Nothing is impossible with God."*[2] It is true. You can do it.

Of course, it will require effort on your part. You will need to be serious about learning God's way of handing money. You may need to become more disciplined in your spending. But I promise you, it will be worth it! Oh, will it be worth it!

Let me acquaint you with Crown Financial Ministries. Crown is a non-profit organization that exists to help you. In 2005, Crown taught about ten million people worldwide what you are going to learn in this book. Our radio programs are broadcast on more than one thousand stations in the United States. Crown also works with tens of thousands of churches to help their members learn God's way of handling money.

Since starting Crown in 1985, I've served as a full-time volunteer receiving no salary or book royalties. The reason I have given my life to this work and am passionate about you learning what the Bible says about money is simple: I want you to enjoy true financial freedom.

Let me encourage you. We've all made mistakes with money in the past—I certainly have made more than my share! Do not let a sense of guilt paralyze or overwhelm you; rather, learn from the experience. The apostle Paul said it this way, *"Forgetting what is behind and straining toward what is ahead, I press on toward the goal."*[3] I want you to press on toward the goal of true financial freedom.

THE ANSWER

Increasingly, people wonder where they can turn for financial advice. There are two basic choices: the Bible and the answers people come up with. The way most people handle money is completely contrary to God's financial principles. The Lord tells us, *"My thoughts are not your thoughts, neither are your ways my ways."*[4]

This book will use the Crown Money Map™ to provide you a simple, proven way to navigate your own journey to true financial freedom—freedom that comes from getting out of debt, increasing your giving and savings, and most importantly, drawing closer to Christ. Remember, the principles you will be learning are a gift from a loving God—a gift intended to benefit you.

A QUESTION FROM MATT

Matt interrupted me, "But what about the problems in our economy? How are they going to impact us in the future?"

"That's right," Jennifer added. "Too many people we know have lost their jobs to cheap labor overseas. Prices seem to be going up on everything, and salaries just aren't keeping up with inflation. From what I hear, the government is going deeper and deeper in debt. Something's gotta give, and I'm afraid it's going to hurt."

I looked across the table at the Mitchells and said, "Your concerns are justified. Most people sense there are giant problems in our economy that could affect us all. This is another reason why you need to be really serious about applying God's principles now. Don't wait until things get worse. Although God's way of handling money works regardless of what's happening in the economy, it's much easier to make progress on your financial journey when the economy is in good shape.

"Well, let's take a look at your financial statement," I said.

Matt glanced at Jennifer and reluctantly slid the paper across the table. My eyes went to the bottom line and saw a negative net worth of $21,720.

FINANCIAL STATEMENT
Matt and Jennifer Mitchell

Assets (what I/we own)

Cash on hand/Checking account	500
Savings	1,200
Stocks and bonds	500
Cash value of life insurance	0
Coins	0
Home	205,000
Other real estate	0
Mortgages/Notes receivable	0
Business valuation	0
Automobiles	19,200
Furniture	3,000
Jewelry	700
Other personal property	2,000
Pension/Retirement accounts	16,350
Other assets	0
Total Assets:	248,450

Liabilities (what I/we owe)

Credit card debt	17,230
Automobile loans	23,640
Home mortgage	177,600
Other real estate mortgages	0
Debts to relatives	0
Business loans	0
Student loans	19,200
Medical/past-due bills	0
Life insurance loans	0
Bank loans	32,500
Other debts and loans	0
Total Liabilities:	270,170
Net Worth (assets minus liabilities)	($ 21,720)

After glancing at the statement, I said, "Let's get together in about a week. I'll study this. Now I'd like you to do three things before we meet."

THE ASSIGNMENT

"One of the reasons I wanted you to complete a financial statement is to determine if there's anything you don't really *need* that might be sold to help you make faster progress on your journey. Ask yourselves this hard question about everything you have: Do we really need it? If not, consider selling it. You can use the money to pay off debt and build up your savings.

"Second," I continued, "keep track of every penny you both spend for the next thirty days. Carry some paper with you and write down *everything* you spend to give you an accurate idea of what you're actually spending. This is the first step in developing a Spending Plan, which you'll start at Destination 1.

"Then get together each day to review what you spent and record it. Begin each of these meetings by praying for each other. As you might have guessed, this can be an emotional time. I want you to love and encourage each other through it.

"Third, study the Crown Money Map," I said, handing it to them. "This is the map you'll follow on your journey to true financial freedom.

"Bev and I will coach you every step of the way. And never forget: The Lord will be with you through the entire journey."

YOUR ASSIGNMENT

The assignment I gave to Matt and Jennifer is *your* assignment, too. You need to get a firm grip on the reality of your situation. There is a blank Financial Statement on page 28. If you haven't already completed a similar one, please complete it.

Also, begin writing down everything you spend for thirty days. Then you'll be ready to complete your own Spending Plan and make some real progress on the journey to *true financial freedom.*

Roadside Assistance—Online!

Personality ID. Want to know your money personality? What are the financial strengths and weaknesses of your personality type? To find out this helpful information, take the Crown Money Map Personality ID online. Remember, *Roadside Assistance—Online!* is free. Log on to **CrownMoneyMap.org.**

Financial statements. Visit CrownMoneyMap.org to print off blank 8½ x 11 Financial Statements.

Income and spending sheet. A helpful online form is available for you to keep track of your income and spending for the next thirty days.

FINANCIAL STATEMENT

Assets (what I/we own)

Cash on hand/Checking account	_____
Savings	_____
Stocks and bonds	_____
Cash value of life insurance	_____
Coins	_____
Home	_____
Other real estate	_____
Mortgages/Notes receivable	_____
Business valuation	_____
Automobiles	_____
Furniture	_____
Jewelry	_____
Other personal property	_____
Pension/Retirement accounts	_____
Other assets	_____

Total Assets: _____

Liabilities (what I/we owe)

Credit card debt	_____
Automobile loans	_____
Home mortgage	_____
Other real estate mortgages	_____
Debts to relatives	_____
Business loans	_____
Student loans	_____
Medical/past-due bills	_____
Life insurance loans	_____
Bank loans	_____
Other debts and loans	_____

Total Liabilities: _____

Net Worth (assets minus liabilities) _____

The journey of a thousand miles begins with one step.

— ANONYMOUS

YOUR MONEY MAP

We invited the Mitchells to our home for dinner. Over the meal, Matt and Jennifer told us they were feeling financial hope for the first time in a long time. They realized the journey they were about to begin was one of the most important steps of their married life, and they could feel their relationship improving. The stress and hopelessness of financial bondage were gradually being replaced by the hope of financial freedom.

Matt recognized that Jennifer had a need for financial stability, that she felt more secure in their marriage when their finances were in good shape. And Jennifer told how she had started to think of ways to cut expenses instead of spending and complaining.

After the meal, Matt spread a copy of the Crown Money Map™ on the table. "We're finding it easier to discuss our finances without fighting. And now that we have the Money Map, we have a clear picture of what to do next."

"It's the journey Bev and I have been on for more than thirty years," I responded. "As I mentioned in our last meeting, we started with a mountain of debt, little savings, and we weren't generous givers. How we each thought about money and spent it strained our marriage terribly. We had no clue that the Bible said so much about it.

"Once we learned God's way of handling money, we wanted to work toward true financial freedom. In other words, we wanted to get in a position where we didn't need to earn a salary to meet our needs. We wanted to be able to volunteer part or all of our time to serve our church or a ministry without having to receive a wage if that's where the Lord wanted us to work.

"As great as that goal sounded, it seemed totally unrealistic, and we had all kinds of questions. Where should we start? What should we do next? How could we stay motivated for so long? These challenges were amplified because our finances were in such poor shape.

"We also knew this would take a *loooong* time and require a lot of effort, but that by God's grace it was possible."

I explained that eventually I stumbled across the "steady plodding" principle. The Bible says, *"Steady plodding brings prosperity."*[1] The original Hebrew words for *steady plodding* pictures a person filling a large barrel one handful at a time. Little by little the barrel is filled to overflowing.

"This was the way we could reach true financial freedom" I told Matt and Jennifer. "We needed to have a plan with a series of small, achievable steps along the way. And we always needed to focus on accomplishing the next step on the journey no matter what challenges we faced. We lived what has become the Crown Money Map. And it works!"

THE CROWN MONEY MAP

Crown Financial Ministries developed the Money Map to help people on their journey toward true financial freedom. It is easy to understand and follow, and is a proven, step-by-step guide that works for *everyone* regardless of your financial situation. You may not reach the final destination, but you can make progress. And I have good news for you: Each destination along the way brings you greater freedom, peace, stability, and even joy.

THE JOURNEY TO TRUE FINANCIAL FREEDOM

Find your destination.

A color foldout containing the seven destinations is attached to the inside back cover. Open the foldout and look at the seven destinations on the journey, also shown on the next two pages.

Take a few minutes and review each destination. Check off the boxes that you've already accomplished. Then start with the first destination you have not yet finished. For example, you may already have purchased your home but not paid off your credit cards. Check off the home purchase box at Destination 5 and then start at Destination 2, working to eliminate credit card debt. Complete each destination in order before proceeding to the next.

As with any journey, there will be bumps in the road, detours, unexpected setbacks, and decisions to make. Some people will make the trip faster than others. You will reach some of your destinations quickly; other destinations may take much longer. But it's worth the effort and even the sacrifices you'll make. Remember, with God's help, you can make real progress.

> **HeyHoward@Crown.org**
>
> **QUESTION:** *Should we sell our home and pay off our credit cards and car loans so that we can complete the destinations in order?*
> **ANSWER:** *It all depends. If you live in an affordable home and can make steady progress on the Money Map, keep it. However, if your home is too expensive and stretches your budget to the breaking point, consider downsizing.*

Pack your bags.

Matt folded up his Money Map as I said, "Before you start a long trip you have to prepare by packing your bags. And before you begin the journey to *true financial freedom,* you need to prepare by learning God's financial principles. It's the most important part of the entire journey.

"When you want to build a home, you need to lay a good foundation because the entire home will rest on it. During our next few meetings, we will look at what God says about money; they are the foundation. After the

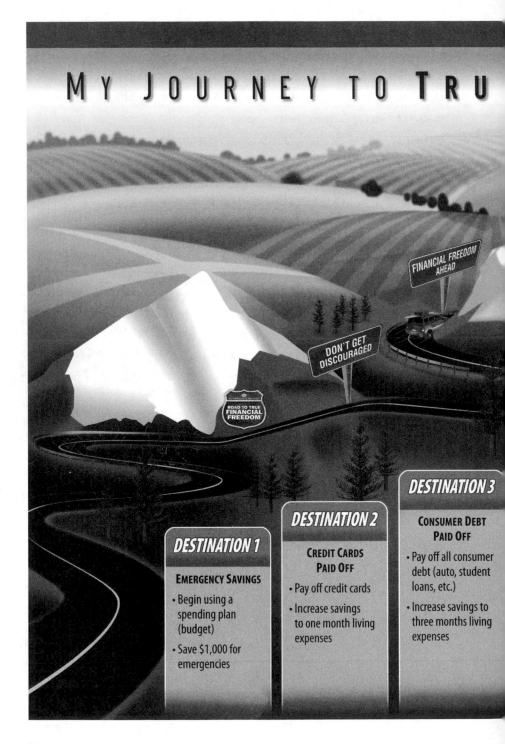

MY JOURNEY TO TRU

FINANCIAL FREEDOM AHEAD

DON'T GET DISCOURAGED

ROAD TO TRUE FINANCIAL FREEDOM

DESTINATION 1

EMERGENCY SAVINGS

- Begin using a spending plan (budget)
- Save $1,000 for emergencies

DESTINATION 2

CREDIT CARDS PAID OFF

- Pay off credit cards
- Increase savings to one month living expenses

DESTINATION 3

CONSUMER DEBT PAID OFF

- Pay off all consumer debt (auto, student loans, etc.)
- Increase savings to three months living expenses

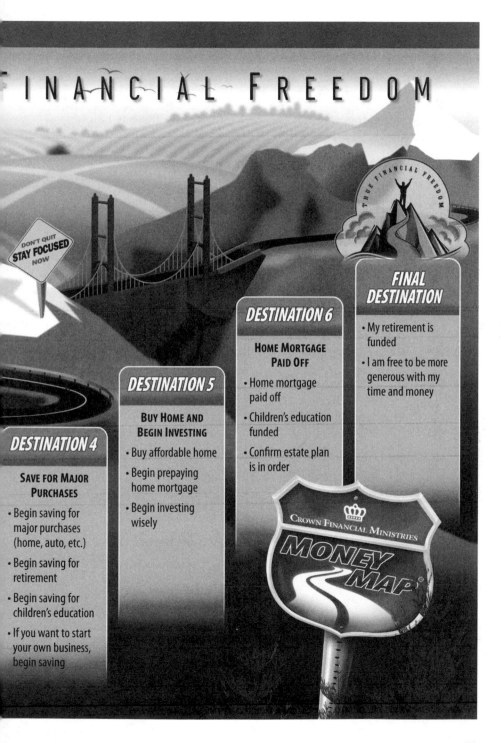

FINANCIAL FREEDOM

DON'T QUIT
STAY FOCUSED
NOW

TRUE FINANCIAL FREEDOM

FINAL DESTINATION

- My retirement is funded
- I am free to be more generous with my time and money

DESTINATION 6

HOME MORTGAGE PAID OFF

- Home mortgage paid off
- Children's education funded
- Confirm estate plan is in order

DESTINATION 5

BUY HOME AND BEGIN INVESTING

- Buy affordable home
- Begin prepaying home mortgage
- Begin investing wisely

DESTINATION 4

SAVE FOR MAJOR PURCHASES

- Begin saving for major purchases (home, auto, etc.)
- Begin saving for retirement
- Begin saving for children's education
- If you want to start your own business, begin saving

CROWN FINANCIAL MINISTRIES

MONEY MAP

foundation, we will build the remainder of the house and apply these principles in very practical ways.

"Next weekend let's go to the park and hang out for a while. I'll begin to teach you God's way of handling money. Oh, and don't forget to keep tracking your spending and income every day. That will really help you as you start on Destination 1."

Roadside Assistance—Online!

HeyHoward@Crown.org. Got a question about money? Each week hundreds of people email me their financial questions at **HeyHoward@Crown.org**. A few I'm able to answer on Crown's radio programs, the rest by e-mail.

Money Map coaching. Receive additional help through free, online Money Map coaching by logging on to **CrownMoneyMap.org**. You can also record your progress and maintain your own personal journey to true financial freedom by using the trip log on the Web site.

*Everything in the heavens and earth is yours,
O Lord, and this is your kingdom. We adore you
as being in control of everything. Riches and honor
come from you alone, and you are the ruler of all
mankind; your hand controls power and might,
and it is at your discretion that men are made
great and given strength.*

— KING DAVID

CHAPTER 4

WHO'S THE REAL OWNER?

It was a sunny day when we met Matt and Jennifer at the park the following weekend. As we headed for a shaded spot, Matt said, "I've been thinking about one of the things you told us. It's been bothering me all week."

"Only one thing?" I said smiling.

Matt's expression relaxed as he continued. "You said something about thousands of verses in the Bible relating to money and that Jesus talked about it more than almost any other subject. I just don't get it. After all, Jesus never had to use a checkbook or even face the temptations of using credit cards."

"Great question, Matt," I chuckled. "I've thought a lot about that, too. God said so much about money for two reasons.

"First, how we handle our money impacts the closeness of our relationship with Him. Jesus said, *'If you have not been faithful in handling worldly wealth, who will trust you with true riches?'* [1] Have you ever thought about what those true riches are? They're all about knowing God well, and there is nothing greater in life than that. I've discovered that every time I apply one of God's financial principles, I grow closer to Him.

"This may surprise you, but money is the primary competitor with God for our affection. Jesus tells us we will serve—and love—one or the other. *'No one can serve two masters; for either he will hate the one and love the other, or he will be devoted to the one and despise the other. You cannot serve both God and Money.'*[2]

How we handle our money impacts the closeness of our relationship with God. Every time you apply one of God's financial principles, you will grow closer to Him.

"When the Crusades were fought during the twelfth century, the Crusaders purchased the services of mercenaries to fight for them. Because it was a religious war, the Crusaders insisted that the mercenaries be baptized before fighting.

"As they were being baptized, the soldiers would take their swords and hold them up out of the water to symbolize that Jesus Christ was not in control of their swords, that they retained the freedom to use their weapons in any way they wished.

"Many people today do a similar thing. They hold their wallet or purse *out of the water*, an attitude that says, 'God, I yield control of my entire life to you except in the area of money—I am perfectly capable of handling that myself.' And without realizing it, this attitude hinders their relationship with God."

"That makes sense," Matt said, nodding his head.

I continued. "The second reason God says so much about money is that He wants to equip us to handle it wisely. He realizes that money plays a big part in our lives. We spend much of our time working for it, deciding how to spend it, grappling with debt, thinking about where to save and invest it, and praying about giving it. The Lord knew money would be a challenge—even a source of conflict—for many of us. And because God loves us, He graciously gave us these financial principles."

WHO'S RESPONSIBLE AROUND HERE?

There is a division of responsibilities in the handling of money. Simply put, God has certain responsibilities and has given others to us. Most of the frustration we experience in our finances comes from not realizing which responsibilities are ours and which are not. In this chapter we'll look at God's responsibilities; in chapter 5 we'll look at ours.

> *God knew money would be a challenge—even a source of conflict—for many of us. And because God loves us, he graciously gave us His financial principles.*

God's Responsibilities

God has three primary responsibilities with money and possessions.

1. God owns all your possessions. He created all things and owns everything. The Bible says, *"The earth is the LORD's, and everything in it."*[3] God even identifies Himself as the owner of specific things: *"The land is mine,"*[4] *"the silver is mine and the gold is mine,"*[5] and *"every animal of the forest is mine, and the cattle on a thousand hills . . . and the creatures of the field are mine. If I were hungry I would not tell you, for the world is mine, and all that is in it."*[6]

When we acknowledge God's ownership, every spending decision becomes a spiritual decision. No longer do we ask, "Lord, what do you want me to do with my money?" The question is restated, "Lord, what do you want me to do with *Your* money?" When we have this attitude, spending, saving, and investing decisions are equally as spiritual as giving decisions.

One of the reasons it is difficult to recognize God's ownership consistently is because He has chosen to be invisible to us. It is easy to believe intellectually that God owns all we have yet still live as if this were not true. Since our culture continually suggests that we own our possessions, we need a total change of mind-set to embrace God's ownership.

2. God is in control. Besides being owner, God ultimately controls every event. The Bible says, *"The LORD does whatever pleases him, in the heavens and on the earth."*[7] King David worshiped God, saying, *"We adore you as being in*

HeyHoward@Crown.org

QUESTION: *I'm totally frustrated! God says He's going to provide my needs. So, what's there for me to do? Do I have to go to work?*

ANSWER: *God has certain responsibilities when it comes to money and He's given others to us. He's promised to provide our needs and at the same time He wants us to work hard—for many reasons. He usually provides our needs through our work.*

control of everything."[8]

It is important to realize that our heavenly Father orchestrates even devastating circumstances for ultimate good in the lives of godly people. The Bible says, *"We know that God causes all things to work together for good to those who love God, to those who are called according to His purpose."*[9]

The Lord allows difficult circumstances for three reasons:

• ***To accomplish His intentions.*** This is illustrated in the life of Joseph, who was sold into slavery as a teenager by his own brothers and later promoted to prime minister of Egypt. Joseph told his brothers: *"Do not be angry with yourselves for selling me here, because it was to save lives that God sent me. . . . It was not you who sent me here, but God. . . . You intended to harm me, but God intended it for good to accomplish what is now being done."*[10]

• ***To develop our character.*** Godly character is precious in the sight of the Lord. He often uses trying times—our best teacher—to develop it in us. The Bible says, *"We also rejoice in our sufferings, because we know that suffering produces perseverance; perseverance, character."*[11]

• ***To discipline us.*** Just as a loving father corrects his child, we can expect our loving heavenly Father to discipline us when we need it. *"The Lord disciplines those he loves. . . . God disciplines us for our good, that we may share in his holiness."*[12] Sometimes this affects our finances. However, His discipline is always for our ultimate benefit and administered out of infinite love.

You can be at peace, knowing that your loving heavenly Father is in control of every situation you will ever face, and that He intends to use each of them for a good purpose.

3. God provides our needs. God's third responsibility is His promise to provide our needs. Jesus said, *"Seek first his kingdom and his righteousness, and all these things* [food and clothing] *will be given to you as well.* "[13]

The same Lord who fed manna forty years[14] to the children of Israel during their wandering in the wilderness and who fed five thousand with only five loaves of bread and two fish[15] has promised to provide our needs.

Concerning our needs, *God is both predictable and unpredictable.* He is totally predictable in His faithfulness to provide for our needs. What we cannot predict is *how* the Lord will provide. He uses different and sometimes surprising means—perhaps a gift or an increase in income. He may provide an opportunity to stretch limited resources through money-saving purchases. Regardless of how He chooses to provide for our needs, He is completely reliable.

It is important to understand the difference between a need and a want. A need is a *basic necessity of life:* food, clothing, or shelter. A want is *anything in excess of a need.* The Lord may allow us to have our wants, but He has not promised to provide them all.

GETTING TO KNOW GOD

God, as He is revealed in the Bible, differs greatly from the way most people imagine Him. Our tendency is to shrink God down and fit Him into a mold with human abilities and limitations. This influences the way we think He can be involved in our finances. We do not understand the greatness of God *"who stretched out the heavens and laid the foundations of the earth."* [16] Learning what the Bible tells us about God expands our perspective of him. Consider just a few examples.

He is Lord of the universe.

God's abilities are beyond our understanding. Astronomers estimate that there are more than 100 billion galaxies in the universe, each containing billions of stars. Though our sun is a relatively small star, it could contain over one million earths. The prophet Isaiah said, *"Lift up your eyes on high and see who has created these stars ... He calls them all by name; because of the greatness of His might and the strength of His power, not one of them is missing."* [17]

He is Lord of the individual.

God is intimately involved with each of us as individuals. *"You are familiar with all my ways. Before a word is on my tongue you know it completely, O LORD. . . . All the days ordained for me were written in your book before one of them came to be."*[18] The Lord is so involved in our lives that He reassures us, *"The very hairs of your head are all numbered."*[19] Our heavenly Father is the one who knows us the best and loves us the most.

> *Our heavenly Father is the one who knows us the best and loves us the most.*

God hung the stars in space and fashioned the earth's towering mountains and mighty oceans. Jeremiah observed correctly, *"Nothing is too hard for you."*[20] Yet God is personally interested in your financial life. Nothing in this book is more important than catching the vision of who God is and what His responsibilities are in our finances.

"Wow!" said Jennifer. "I didn't understand how much God is involved in our financial life. But it seems as if He does it all. Is there anything left for us to do?

"I'm so glad you asked," Bev answered with a twinkle in her eyes. "Let's grab something to eat and talk about it."

Roadside Assistance—Online!

Crown radio. Learn more about what God says about handling money by listening to our radio programs. Log on to **CrownMoneyMap.org** to find the stations nearest you, or listen online 24/7 or Podcast the programs.

Online Money Map community. Join the online Money Map community and share your own videos or written insights, challenges, and celebrations with others on the journey.

*Jesus Christ said more about money than any other
single thing because money is of first importance when
it comes to a person's real character.*

— RICHARD HALVERSON

Former chaplain of United States Senate

WE ARE MANAGERS

After we finished eating our sandwiches, Bev suggested, "Let's go for a walk and talk about our financial responsibilities."

"Great idea," Jennifer said as Matt nodded approval. "There's a beautiful waterfall less than a mile away."

"Let's go for it!" Bev said, pointing the way.

As the four of us walked, I picked up where we had left off in our earlier discussion. "As you've already learned," I began, "God's role as owner covers the biggest issues.

"The word in the Bible that best describes our role is *steward*. A steward is a manager of someone else's possessions. Our responsibility is summed up in a verse that says: '*It is required of stewards that one be found faithful.*'[1]

"Before we can be faithful, we must know what we're required to do. Just as the purchaser of a complicated piece of machinery studies the manufacturer's manual to learn how to operate it, we need to examine the Creator's handbook—the Bible—to determine how He wants us to handle His possessions."

FOUR KEY RESPONSIBILITIES

Then I told Jennifer and Matt what we must all remember:

The more you learn to handle money God's way, the more likely He is to entrust you with more. And I want that for you. You have four responsibilities that are important for you to understand.

1. Be faithful with what you have.

God wants us to be faithful regardless of how much we have. Jesus told a parable about money to illustrate this. *"It will be like a man going on a journey, who called his servants and entrusted his property to them. To one he gave five talents* [a sum] *of money, to another two talents."*[2]

> *"The world applauds success; God applauds faithfulness."*
>
> ANONYMOUS

When the man returned, he praised the faithful servant for his management of the five talents: *"Well done, good and faithful servant. You were faithful with a few things, I will put you in charge of many things; enter into the joy of your master."*[3] Interestingly, the servant who had been given two talents and the one who had been given five talents received the identical reward. God rewards *faithfulness* regardless of the amount.

We are required to be faithful whether we have much or little. As someone once said, "It's not what I would do if one million dollars were my lot; it's what I am doing with the ten dollars I've got."

2. Be faithful with 100 percent.

God wants us to be faithful in handling all of our money. Unfortunately, most Christians have been taught how to handle only 10 percent of their income God's way—the area of giving. And although this area is crucial, so is the other 90 percent, which most people have learned to handle from the world's perspective.

However, the Bible gives us guidance on how to earn, spend, give, save, invest, get out of debt, and teach our children how to handle money. In short, everything you need to know about handling money wisely is found in the Bible. The wheel below illustrates our responsibilities.

Since most people have not been equipped to handle 100 percent of their money God's way, many of them have wrong attitudes toward possessions. This often leads to incorrect financial decisions and painful consequences. God correctly observed, "*My people are destroyed from lack of knowledge.*"[4]

3. Be faithful in little things.

Jesus said, "*He who is faithful in a very little thing is faithful also in much.*"[5] This is critical for you to understand. If you have the character to be faithful with small financial things, God knows that He can trust you with greater things. Missionary statesman Hudson Taylor

STARTLING STATS:

Most people have been taught how to handle 10 percent of their income God's way but don't know what He wants them to do with the other 90 percent.

said it this way, "Small things are small things, but *faithfulness* with a small thing is a big thing."

Think about it. How do you know if a child is going to take good care of his first car? Observe how he cared for his bicycle. How do you know if a salesperson will do a competent job of serving a large client? Evaluate how she served a small client. If you spend small amounts wisely, God knows He can trust you with more.

> *"Small things are small things, but faithfulness with a small thing is a big thing."*
>
> HUDSON TAYLOR

Some people become frustrated by the inability to solve their financial problems quickly. They abandon the goal of becoming debt free or increasing their saving or giving because the task looks impossible. And sometimes the task *is* impossible without God's help. Your job is to make a genuine effort, no matter how small it may appear, and then leave the results to God. I love what God said, *"Do not despise these small beginnings."* [6] Don't be discouraged. Be faithful to do what you can—even though it may seem insignificant.

4. Be faithful with other people's stuff.

Faithfulness with another's possessions will, in some measure, determine how much you are given. The Bible says, *"If you have not been faithful in the use of that which is another's, who will give you that which is your own?"* [7]

This is often overlooked. Ask yourself these questions. Are you careless with your employer's office supplies? When someone allows you to use something, do you return it in good shape? I am certain that God has not entrusted more to some because they have been unfaithful with others' possessions.

MATT'S RESPONSE

"So those are our responsibilities," Matt said. "We're to be faithful with what we have. We're to be faithful in handling all our income and not just what we give. And we're to be faithful even with small things."

"Yes, you've got it, Matt," I said.

Matt massaged his eyebrows as though he had a headache. "Well, there's one thing I still don't understand. Some people say Christians should always be rich while others disagree and think the only way to stay close to Christ is to be poor. What's the Bible say?"

"The Bible teaches neither. It says that we have the responsibility to be faithful stewards. Let me draw you a chart that contrasts three different views to help you understand.

Three Attitudes toward Possessions

	POVERTY	STEWARDSHIP	PROSPERITY
Possessions are	Evil	A responsibility	A right
I work to	Meet only basic needs	Serve Christ	Become rich
Godly people are	Poor	Faithful	Wealthy
Ungodly people are	Wealthy	Unfaithful	Poor
I give	Because I must	Because I love God	To get
My spending is	Without gratitude to God	Prayerful and responsible	Carefree and consumptive

"And, Matt, there's one other thing that's helpful to understand," I said. "All through the Bible there is a correlation between the development of our character and how we handle money. You've heard the expression, 'Money talks.' And it does, because we spend our money on the things that are most important to us. You can tell more about our character and priorities by examining our checkbook and credit card statement than by listening to us talk.

"God uses money to refine our character," I said as I fumbled through my backpack for a book I was currently reading. "Let me read something David McConaugh wrote in this book entitled *Money, the Acid Test.* Even though it was published in 1918, it's just as true today."

"'Money, most common of temporal things, involves uncommon and eternal consequences. Even though it may be done quite unconsciously, money molds people in the process of getting it, saving it, spending it, and giving it. Depending on how you use it, it proves to be a blessing or a curse. Either you become master of the money or the money becomes the master of you. The Lord takes money, as essential as it is to our common life, and uses it to test our lives and as an instrument to mold us into the likeness of himself.'[7]

HeyHoward@Crown.org

QUESTION: *I thought the Bible says that if I give generously, God is supposed to prosper me. Why hasn't this happened? I'm confused.*

ANSWER: *It's important that you handle **all** your money God's way. Some people are generous but suffer financially because they're dishonest or they don't work hard or they use credit to spend more than they can afford.*

"Now, that's powerful," Matt said, scratching his head. "I've never thought about God using money to develop our character."

"It certainly changed the way I view using money," I agreed. "Why don't we start walking back, and let me give you two an assignment."

THE MITCHELLS' ASSIGNMENT

"I want you to go through the exercise of transferring the ownership of your possessions to God. I've got a deed to help you to do this because a deed is often used to transfer the ownership of property."

I handed it to Matt and continued, "The deed isn't legally binding. We've discovered that when the deed is completed, people become more serious about acknowledging God's ownership. This is important because we all occasionally forget that God owns everything we have. So complete the deed together. Take your time and pray. Really think about what you are doing."

"This sounds like a super idea," Matt responded enthusiastically. "I notice there are a couple of spaces at the bottom of the deed for witnesses. Why don't we get together next week when Jennifer and I have filled it out, and the two of you can witness it for us."

"We'd love to!" I answered. "And while we're together, I'll tell you what the Bible says about giving."

YOUR ASSIGNMENT

Follow these steps to complete the blank deed on page 54:

1. Insert today's date.

2. Print your name. You are the one transferring ownership.

3. The Lord is the one receiving the assets.

4. Prayerfully consider what possessions you want to list, acknowledging God's ownership.

5. Sign your name.

6. Ask one or two friends to witness your deed, signing on the lines at the bottom.

BEV'S INSIGHTS

Completing the deed was a statement of trust for us: We were trusting God with the ownership of everything we had. Instead of being painful, it was a relief to realize that we were simply managers of whatever God entrusted to us—including our children.

I am convinced that God did not create us to shoulder the heavy responsibilities and burdens of ownership. That's His role. Jesus said it this way: *"Come to me, all you who are weary and burdened, and I will give you rest. . . . For my yoke is easy and my burden is light."*[8]

Until we realize that we were made to be stewards and not owners, we will never experience *true financial freedom*.

Roadside Assistance—Online!

The Deed. If you would like a larger copy of the deed to display as a reminder, visit **CrownMoneyMap.org** to print one.

Deed

This Deed, Made the _____ day of _____

From: _____

To: The Lord

I (we) hereby transfer to God the ownership of the following possessions:

Witnesses who hold me (us) accountable
in the recognition of the Lord's ownership:

_____

_____

Stewards of the possessions above:

_____

_____

This instrument is not a binding legal document.

MAKING PROGRESS ON THE JOURNEY

Ambition had always dominated my life—the ambition to become very rich. I was never a planner, preferring instead to follow my impulses. I had no map for achieving my goal, and I rarely accepted advice or considered the consequences. Bad investment deals led to living on loans, postdated checks, unemployment, and deep debt.

A job offer moved me, along with my wife and three children, to a new city where we heard about Crown. Desperate for change, we jumped at the chance to get into Crown's small group study. Suddenly confronted with a financial map we could follow, we discovered that we'd been doing it all wrong.

For the first time in our lives, we decided to stop living on credit. We are paying off all of our debts one by one and setting aside money for emergencies.

We sold our financed car, which meant my wife had to ride a bicycle to work. Even though she was in favor of the decision, the reality wasn't easy. One dark morning as she pedaled to work in the cold, the Lord spoke to her heart, reminding her what the apostle Paul said in the Bible, *"I have learned to be content in whatever circumstances I am."*

God has convinced us that He will supply all of our needs but not necessarily all of our wants; He wants us to trust in and depend on Him. We have taught these same truths to our children, who are learning to give, save, and spend according to God's design.

The biggest life changer for me was the Lord's perspective on eternity. Even if I achieved my old goal of becoming rich and buying everything I wanted, it would get me nowhere because this life is so short! Now we enjoy God's blessing as we live with eternity in view.

—WALDINEI AND LUCIANY BUENO, *South America*

*Read and watch more stories along the journey at **CrownMoneyMap.org**.*

DISCUSSION QUESTIONS

1. Where are you on the Money Map—what destinations have you completed? What do you want to accomplish by reading this book?

2. What personal challenge(s) do you feel after learning the reasons the Bible says so much about money?

3. Do you consistently recognize that God is the owner of all your possessions? What will you do to help recognize His ownership?

4. Why is it important to realize that God uses even difficult circumstances for ultimate good? Share a difficult circumstance you have experienced and how the Lord used it for good.

5. What challenged your thinking about what it means to be a faithful steward? In what way?

6. Are you faithful in handling all of your money God's way? If not, in what areas do you need to improve?

TOOLS FOR YOUR JOURNEY

Here are several tools that will help you discover God's way of handling money:

- *Crown small group study.* I've taught more than fifty of these ten-week studies. They are one of the most powerful and effective ways to learn God's financial principles. One major benefit of the small group is that close relationships are developed among the participants.

- *Journey to True Financial Freedom seminar.* This one-day live seminar sponsored by Crown Financial Ministries is taught around the country.

- *Your Money Map book on CD.* An abridged audio of this book is available that can reinforce what you read here. Whether you listen at home or in your car, you can review these key financial principles. The audio book is available at your local Christian retailer or **CrownMoneyMap.org**.

- *Your Money Map Workshop* **on DVD.** Six encouraging DVD video lessons that go step-by-step with this book are available for personal or small group study. For details, visit your local Christian retailer or the Web site **Crown MoneyMap.org**.

- *The New Master Your Money* (Chicago: Moody, 2004) is an outstanding book written by CPA and financial planning expert Ron Blue.

PART

2

PACK YOUR BAGS *for the* JOURNEY

It is more blessed to give than to receive.
—JESUS CHRIST

GIVING

After we witnessed Matt and Jennifer's signatures on their deed, I asked Matt a question.

"Matt, what do you think about giving? Last week at the park, I noticed that your smile disappeared the moment I mentioned it."

After a deep sigh, he began. "This is hard," he said. "I have so many mixed feelings."

"Sounds like you may have some of the same questions and struggles as Howard when he first wrestled with giving," Bev said.

Matt laughed. "Well, it's not that I don't want to give," he said. "Although I probably *don't* want to give as much as Jennifer. In fact, we've argued about it, but I just feel like we can't afford it right now. With our financial situation like it is, it just wouldn't be responsible."

"Well, I've got good news for you, Matt. First, you're ahead of where I was; at least you *want* to give," I reasoned. "Second, once you really understand God's truth about giving, you'll find that it's a huge blessing. God has designed giving to be an exciting journey that will increase your faith in Him.

And, I know this may sound radical, but you'll experience real joy as you give."

Matt glanced at me, his mouth beginning to form a faint smile. "No kidding? It can really work like that?"

"It can and it will," I said. "I know from experience. At first I would go to almost any length to avoid giving. However, once I learned what God said about it, I wanted to give; but then I had a different problem—I was convinced we couldn't afford it.

"But we started giving, and over time I've gained more and more confidence in God's faithfulness.

"However, no sooner did we get over that hurdle than we had to face another one: an unlimited number of needs and our very limited resources. How could we decide to whom to give? Our local church, the hungry poor, missionary efforts—all kinds of genuine needs looking for financial support.

"So let's examine what the Bible says about giving in three areas: attitude, advantages, and amount."

OUR ATTITUDE IN GIVING

God's attitude in giving is summed up in this verse: *"For God so loved the world that he gave his one and only Son."*[1] Note the sequence. Because God loved, He gave. Because *God is love*[2], He is also a giver. He set the example of giving motivated by love.

It's also crucial for *us* to give with an attitude of love. The Bible says, *"If I give all my possessions to feed the poor . . . but do not have love, it profits me nothing."*[3] It is hard to imagine anything more commendable than giving everything to the poor. But if it is done without love, it is of no benefit to the giver.

In God's economy the attitude is even more important than the amount. Jesus emphasized this point: *"Woe upon you, Pharisees, and you other religious leaders—hypocrites! For you tithe* [give 10 percent] *down to the last mint leaf in your garden, but ignore the important things—justice and mercy and faith."*[4]

The religious leaders had been careful to give precisely the correct amount. Yet, in spite of this, Christ rebuked them because of their attitude.

For giving to be of any value, it must be done from a heart of love.

The only way we can consistently give out of love is to give our gifts to the Lord Himself. If giving is merely to a church, a ministry, or a needy person, it is only charity. But giving to God becomes an act of worship. Because He is our Creator, our Savior, and our faithful provider, we can express our gratefulness and love by giving to Him. Whenever we give, we should remind ourselves that we are giving our gift to the Lord Himself.

Stop. Examine yourself. What is your attitude toward giving?

"The world will never be won to Christ with what people can conveniently share."

BERNARD EDINGER

ADVANTAGES OF GIVING

Obviously a gift benefits the recipient. The church continues its ministry, the hungry are fed, and missionaries are sent. However, if a gift is given with the proper attitude, the giver, surprisingly, benefits even more. *"Remember the words of the Lord Jesus, that He Himself said, 'It is more blessed to give than to receive.'"*[5] The giver receives three extraordinary benefits.

1. Increase in Intimacy

Above all else, giving increases our affection for Christ. The Bible says, *"Where your treasure is, there your heart will be also."*[6] This is why it is necessary to give each gift to Jesus Christ. When you give your gift to Him, your heart will *automatically* be drawn to Him. And nothing in life compares to knowing Christ well.

In some mysterious way we cannot fully comprehend, Jesus Christ, the Creator of all things, personally identifies Himself with the poor. When we give to the poor we are actually giving to Jesus.

2. Increase in Heaven

Jesus wants us to know that when we give, we are investing treasures in heaven that we will be able to enjoy for *all eternity*. He told us, *"Store up for yourselves treasures in heaven, where moth and rust do not destroy, and where thieves do not break in and steal.* "[7]

Imagine that you've been offered a high-paying job for two years in

Switzerland, but there's a catch. At the end of two years, you have to leave behind all your Swiss currency and everything you've purchased. The only money you can keep is what you have converted to U.S. dollars and sent home.

So what do you do with your Swiss currency? If you're smart, you'll keep

"What's this we hear about you laying up treasures in heaven?"
Reprinted from *The Saturday Evening Post* magazine, © 1983, Saturday Evening Post Society. Used by permission.

only enough Swiss currency to meet your needs, and you'll convert the rest to American dollars and send it home.

Something similar to this will happen when you die—you'll leave everything behind. And while it is true that you can't take it with you when you die, you can send it on ahead! Paul wrote to some contributors, *"Not that I am looking for a gift, but I am looking for what may be credited to your account."* [8] We each have an account in something comparable to the First National Bank of Heaven. Every time we give, we are making deposits to a heavenly account that is ours to enjoy forever.

3. Increase on Earth

In addition to laying up treasure in heaven, there is a material increase flowing to the giver. The Bible says, *"One man gives freely, yet gains even more; another withholds unduly, but comes to poverty. A generous man will prosper."* [9] Another passage about giving says, *"Whoever sows sparingly will also reap sparingly, and whoever sows generously will also reap generously."* [10]

As shown in the diagram, there is a cycle in giving. God produces an increase so we may give more *and* have our needs met.

When we give, we should do it with a sense of expectancy—anticipating God to provide an increase even though we have no idea when or how He may choose to do it. In my experience, He can be *very* creative!

Remember that you receive the advantages of giving *only* when you give out of a heart filled with love. This rules out the motive of giving just to get.

THE AMOUNT TO GIVE

Let's survey what the Bible says about how much to give. In the Old Testament, giving a tithe—10 percent of one's income—was required. God reprimanded His people for not tithing: *"Will a man rob God? Yet you rob me. But you ask, 'How do we rob you?'* [By not giving] *tithes and offerings."*[11] The New Testament does not reject the concept of the tithe. It emphasizes giving generously, even sacrificially.

What I like about the tithe is that it is systematic, and the amount is easy to compute. However, a potential danger of tithing is the view that once I have tithed, I have fulfilled *all* my responsibilities to give. For many, the tithe

65

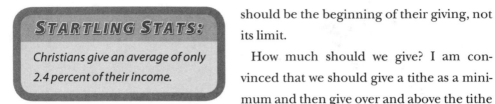

STARTLING STATS:

Christians give an average of only 2.4 percent of their income.

should be the beginning of their giving, not its limit.

How much should we give? I am convinced that we should give a tithe as a minimum and then give over and above the tithe as God prospers or directs us.

PLACES FOR GIVING

People ask Bev and me if we give only through our church. In our case, the answer is no. However, we do give a minimum of 10 percent of our regular income through our church because this is a tangible expression of our commitment to it. We also give to others who are helping us grow spiritually. *"The one who is taught the word is to share all good things with the one who teaches him."*[12]

"That was the best sermon on giving I've ever heard."
© *Rob Portlock.* Used by permission.

In addition, we give to the poor and needy, a kind of giving that clearly pleases God. Paul emphasizes the importance of giving to the needy. *"All they* [the disciples] *asked was that we should continue to remember the poor, the very thing I was eager to do."*[13] And in one of the most stunning passages in the Bible, Jesus tell us: *"I was hungry and you gave me something to eat, I was thirsty and you gave me something to drink . . . whatever you did for one of the least of these brothers of mine, you did for me."*[14]

In some mysterious way we cannot fully comprehend, Jesus Christ, the Creator of all things, personally identifies Himself with the poor. When we give to the poor we are actually giving to Jesus. And if that truth is staggering, then the reciprocal is terrifying: when we do not give to the poor, we leave Christ Himself hungry and thirsty.

HeyHoward@Crown.org

QUESTION: *Should we tithe to our local church?*
ANSWER: *In my opinion you should give at least 10 percent of your income to your church, and then give to other ministries and needs as God directs and provides.*

TAKING A STEP OF FAITH

"Well, Matt and Jennifer, that's a pretty long answer to your question, but I could talk for hours about the benefits of generous, joyful giving. It requires a step of faith when your finances are tight. But you will discover that it can be one of the most exciting and vibrant experiences of your Christian life.

Roadside Assistance—Online!

Read and watch stories about the creative ways that people give in the "Money Map Journey Stories" section at **CrownMoneyMap.org**.

If you love your neighbor as much as you love yourself you will not want to harm or cheat him, or kill him or steal from him. . . . Love does no wrong to anyone.[1]

— THE APOSTLE PAUL

"You shall not steal."

— EIGHTH OF THE TEN COMMANDMENTS

HONESTY

I was expecting the soft knock at the door. Matt Mitchell had called the night before and asked if he could join me for an early morning run. The moment I opened the door, I saw the concern on his face. "What's the matter, Matt?"

"I'll tell you while we run," Matt answered in a hushed voice, "I don't want to wake up your wife."

Jogging down the street, Matt began to unload. "We've got a new salesman at the dealership, and he's outrageously dishonest. He's lying to customers by promising things he can't deliver. He's lying to the sales manager and taking customers from the rest of us. And he's getting away with it! He was the number one salesperson last month."

"I understand your frustration," I said. "And you've nailed the part that is often the hardest to take—the fact that he seems to be getting away with it. But that won't last forever. In the meantime, you need to focus on making sure you do the right thing regardless of what someone else does."

As we continued running and talking, I assured Matt that this is a common problem. All of us must decide whether we will handle money honestly. Do you tell the cashier at the store when you receive too much change? Have you ever been tempted not to tell the whole truth because you might lose a sale?

These decisions are more difficult when so many around us act dishonestly. People today formulate their own standards of honesty, changing them when circumstances change. The Bible speaks of a similar time, when *"every man did what was right in his own eyes."* [2]

> *I believe God will not allow us to keep anything we have acquired dishonestly. The Bible says, "Wealth obtained by fraud dwindles."*

A DANGER TO YOUR FINANCIAL HEALTH

If you are a parent and one of your children steals something, do you allow the child to keep it? Of course not. You require its return because the child's character would be destroyed if he kept it. Not only do you insist on its return, but you probably want the child to experience enough discomfort to produce a lasting impression. For instance, you might have the child confess the theft and ask forgiveness from the store manager.

I believe God will not allow us to keep *anything* we have acquired dishonestly. The Bible says, *"Wealth obtained by fraud dwindles."* [3] Sandra purchased four plants, but the checkout clerk only charged her for one. Sandra knew it but left the store anyway without paying for the other three. She told me, "I couldn't believe how quickly three of the plants died—and the fourth wasn't doing too well, either!"

Remember, dishonesty is dangerous to your financial health.

WHAT GOD SAYS ABOUT HONESTY

There are hundreds of verses in the Bible that communicate God's desire for us to be completely honest. For instance, the Bible says, *"The Lord loathes all cheating and dishonesty,"*[4] and *"The LORD hates . . . a lying tongue,"*[5] and *"You shall not steal."*[6]

Study this comparison between what the Bible teaches and what our society practices concerning honesty.

ISSUE	SCRIPTURE	SOCIETY
Standard of honesty:	Complete honesty	Changes with circumstances
God's concern about honesty:	He requires it	There is no God or He looks the other way
The decision to be honest or dishonest is based upon:	Faith in the invisible, living God	Only facts that can be seen
Question usually asked when deciding whether or not to be honest:	Will it please God?	Will I get away with it?

THE GOD OF TRUTH

Truthfulness is one of God's attributes. He is repeatedly identified as the God of truth. *"I am . . . the truth."*[7] And He commands us to reflect His honest and holy character: *"Be holy yourselves also in all your behavior; because it is written, 'You shall be holy, for I am holy.'"*[8]

God's nature is in utter contrast to Satan's. The Bible describes the devil's character: *"He* [the devil] *was a murderer from the beginning, not holding to the truth, for there is no truth in him . . . for he is a liar and the father of lies."*[9] The Lord wants us to conform to His honest character rather than to the dishonest nature of the devil.

God wants us to be honest for three extremely important reasons.

When being dishonest, we are acting as if God does not even exist.

1. We cannot practice dishonesty and love God.

When being dishonest, we behave as if God were unable to provide exactly what we need even though He has promised to do so. We take the situation into our own hands and do it our own dishonest way. We are also acting as if God is incapable of discovering our dishonesty and is powerless to discipline us. And it is impossible to *"love the Lord your God with all your heart"* [10] when we are acting as if He doesn't even exist!

Honest behavior is an issue of faith. An honest decision may look foolish in light of what we can see. But the godly person knows Jesus Christ is alive even though invisible. Every honest decision strengthens our faith and helps us grow into a closer relationship with Christ. The Bible says it this way, *"The devious are an abomination to the Lord; but He is intimate with the upright."* [11]

2. We cannot practice dishonesty and love our neighbor.

The Bible says, *"If you love your neighbor as much as you love yourself you will not want to harm or cheat him, or kill him or steal from him. . . . Love does no wrong to anyone."* [12] However, when we are dishonest, we are stealing from another person. We may rationalize that it is a business or the government or an insurance company that is suffering loss. Yet, if we look at the bottom line, it is the business owners or fellow taxpayers or policy holders from whom we are stealing. It is just as if we took the money from their wallets. The victim is always a person.

3. Honesty confirms God's direction

The Bible says, *"Put away from you a deceitful mouth and put devious speech far from you . . . and all your ways will be established."* [13] What a tremendous principle. As you are honest, "all your ways will be established." Choosing to walk the narrow path of honesty eliminates the many possible avenues of dishonesty.

"If only I'd understood that," Raymond once told me, "but Donna and I wanted that house so much. It was our dream home. However, we had too much debt to qualify for the mortgage. The only way for us to buy the house was to hide some of our debts from the bank.

"It was the worst decision of our lives. Almost immediately, we were unable to meet the mortgage payment and pay our other debts too. The pressure built and was more than Donna could stand. Our dream home ended up causing a nightmare. I not only lost the home, but nearly lost my wife."

Had Raymond and Donna been honest, the bank would not have approved the loan, and they would have been unable to purchase that particular home. Had they prayed and waited, God may have brought something more affordable, thus avoiding the pressure that almost ended their marriage. Honesty helps confirm God's direction.

HONESTY IN SMALL THINGS

God requires us to be completely honest because even the smallest "white lie" makes our consciences increasingly insensitive to dishonesty. This single cancer cell of dishonesty inevitably multiplies and spreads to greater dishonesty. *"Whoever is dishonest with very little will also be dishonest with much."* [14]

An event in Abraham's life has challenged me to be honest in small matters. The king of Sodom offered him all the goods he recovered when he rescued the people of Sodom. But Abraham responded, *"I have sworn to the Lord God Most High, possessor of heaven and earth, that I will not take a thread or a sandal thong or anything that is yours."* [15]

Just as Abraham was unwilling to take so much as a thread or a sandal thong, I challenge you to make a similar commitment. Decide not to steal a stamp or a photocopy or a paper clip or a long distance telephone call or a penny from your employer, the government, or anyone else. The people of God must be honest in even the smallest matters.

HeyHoward@Crown.org

QUESTION: *Is it permissible to reduce my taxes by using legal tax deductions?*
ANSWER: *Yes! Absolutely! You should use legal tax deductions and pay whatever is due after your deductions.*

R & R: RESTORATION AND RESTITUTION

If we have acquired anything dishonestly, we must return it to its rightful owner and make restitution. *"He shall restore what he took by robbery...or anything about which he swore falsely; he shall make restitution for it in full and add to it one-fifth more. He shall give it to the one to whom it belongs.* "[16]

Restitution is a tangible expression to correct a wrong. God desires us to go beyond mere restitution and add a premium. This has two advantages: It discourages us from repeating the dishonest behavior and it indicates our desire to please God by caring for the person we've injured through our dishonesty. In the Bible, Zaccheus is a good example of fulfilling this principle. He promised Jesus, *"If I have defrauded anyone of anything, I will give back four times as much."* [17]

BRIBES

Bribes are given to influence people to do something wrong or illegal. The taking of bribes is clearly prohibited in the Bible: *"You shall not take a bribe, for a bribe blinds the clear-sighted and subverts the cause of the just."* [18] Bribes are often subtly disguised as "gifts" or "referral fees." Evaluate any such offer you may receive to confirm that it is not really a bribe.

TAXES

"There's one area where I really struggle with being honest," Matt confessed. "It's paying taxes. Most of the guys at work aren't so honest when it comes to taxes. What's God say about this?"

"Someone asked Jesus that very question," I answered. *'Is it right for us to pay taxes to Caesar or not?'* . . . [Jesus said], *'Show me a [Roman coin]. Whose portrait and inscription are on it?'* *'Caesar's,'* they replied. He said to them, *'Then give to Caesar what is Caesar's'"* [19]

This is an example of

"Oh great, now I have to give unto Caesar, too."

© www.CartoonStock.com. Used by permission.

the contrast between what God teaches and what our society practices. The Bible tells us to pay our taxes. *"Everyone must submit himself to the governing authorities, for there is no authority except that which God has established . . . This is also why you pay taxes, for the authorities are God's servants, who give their full time to governing. . . . If you owe taxes, pay taxes."* [20]

Remember, complete honesty on your part is crucial for God to entrust you with resources. It plays a huge part in your financial future.

Roadside Assistance—Online!

Keep track! Continue keeping track of your expenses and experiences on your journey to true financial freedom at **CrownMoneyMap.org**.

"When couples discuss money, it often leads to a fight in which one is accused of spending too much or earning too little. Celebrating progress together develops an attitude of gratitude and promotes healing in a marriage."

— BEVERLY DAYTON

IT'S TIME TO PARTY!

The phone rang at the crack of dawn. Jennifer wanted to speak to Bev, and I could hear she was upset. "Matt has been making progress," Jennifer said with her voice cracking. "But yesterday he bought a couple of shirts, and he already has a closet full of them. I know it sounds like a small thing, but his spending just drives me crazy."

Unfortunately, when couples or individuals think about money or discuss it, often they are dealing with problems. It's not fun. Someone is spending too much or not earning enough income. Frequently it ends in a heated argument, and the whole experience feels negative. We will always face financial challenges, but we can balance this by *celebrating* when good things happen.

CELEBRATE!

This may surprise you. We've learned that celebrating progress on your journey to *true financial freedom* is a key to arriving there. You are much more likely to reach the next destination if you celebrate the one you have just reached.

Did you know that God is not a party pooper? The Bible is loaded with examples of celebrating God's goodness for enabling success. The words *celebrate* and *celebrated* are found 52 times in the Bible.

This is one example from the Old Testament: *"Celebrate the Feast. . . . Be joyful at your Feast. . . . For seven days celebrate the Feast to the LORD your God. . . . For the Lord your God will bless you in all your harvest and in all the work of your hands, and your joy will be complete"*[1]

> **HeyHoward@Crown.org**
>
> **QUESTION:** *My wife and I argue about money all the time, and it's destroying our marriage. What can we do to stop?*
>
> **ANSWER:** *Learn to celebrate, celebrate, celebrate! Celebrate your financial victories every week. Concentrate on affirming each other's strengths and praying together for God's direction and favor on your finances.*

These farmers had worked hard for months. They hoed, planted, watered, weeded, and harvested the crops. Now it was time to celebrate God's faithfulness—time to party! In fact, God *commanded* the people to celebrate because he knew it would be benefit them.

Celebration is part of the fabric of our country. We celebrate our hard-fought independence on July 4th. We celebrate the blessings we have received on Thanksgiving. We celebrate the birth of Christ at Christmas and His resurrection during Easter. Celebration helps us develop a proper attitude of gratitude.

WHY CELEBRATE?

There are several reasons you should celebrate your progress.

Helps You Focus on God

The biggest benefit of celebrating is that it reminds you that God has helped you move forward. Never forget that Jesus said, *"Apart from me you can do nothing."*[2] He has faithfully provided you the opportunities and resources that enabled you to make progress.

Helps You When the Going Gets Tough

Do you think there were times when the farmers became discouraged? The ground was hard; the rains were late, forcing them to irrigate; weeds sprouted up all over the place. These farmers were no strangers to hardship.

Your difficult times are important times to recall previous celebrations. Remembering past victories enables you to look forward to a time when you will rejoice again; it keeps you going when you are tempted to quit. Please engrave this truth in your mind: What you celebrate, you soon will repeat!

When you celebrate progress regularly, it helps you focus on your improvement and not your problems.

Helps You Stay Motivated

Our friends Chuck and Ann were completely out of debt with the exception of their home mortgage. They wanted to pay it off early, but they lacked sufficient motivation to make it happen. Finally, they envisioned how they would celebrate this major accomplishment when they achieved it; they would take their children with them on a white-water camping trip—something they had always wanted to do.

Chuck said, "The prospect of the trip acted like a switch that was finally turned on. It lit our fire! We became serious and started carefully watching our spending so we could apply every spare penny against our home mortgage. The secret was the concept of celebrating."

Helps Your Relationships

Have you ever watched a sports team celebrate after winning a championship? These athletes worked hard, sacrificed, trained, and gave it all they had during the game. No one else really knows the price they paid to win.

STARTLING STATS:

Every 27 seconds a couple in America divorces—totaling about 7,000 divorces a day and affecting some 10,000 children. Money problems play a major role in most of these divorces.

When the final whistle blows and the victory is theirs, what do they do?

79

Grown athletes act like kids! They jump up and down, hug each other, and cry out in pure joy. During the entire process—the hopes, the hardships, the losses, and the final win—they develop the bonds of close friendships with their teammates.

*Let these next five words sink in and revolutionize the way you respond to God and others: Unexpressed gratitude **feels** like ingratitude!*

The same should be true for a married couple, only more so. Instead of allowing money to drive a wedge between you, view money challenges as an *opportunity* to grow closer to each other. Walk down the road to *true financial freedom* together. Communicate well, and when you reach a destination, stop and celebrate!

A close cousin to celebrating is *expressing gratitude*. Let these next five words sink in and revolutionize the way you respond to God and others: Unexpressed gratitude *feels* like ingratitude!

For example, a mother works hours preparing for the Thanksgiving meal, and her family devours the turkey and trimmings in what seems like forty-five seconds! Although they are very grateful for the meal, they fail to say it. This unexpressed gratitude feels like *ingratitude* to the mother. She feels unappreciated, taken for granted.

If you are married, one of the healthiest things you can do for your marriage is to regularly express genuine gratitude to your spouse. Thank your mate for working hard to produce an income. Affirm a wise spending decision. This will help create an environment of mutual encouragement in your family.

HOW OTHERS HAVE DONE IT

One of the keys to celebrating is to pick something you would really like to do or have. Make it a memory; enjoy yourself.

Fortunately, celebration does not have to cost a lot of money. When Bev and I reached Destination 1 on our journey, all we could afford was a visit to the beach nearby. We loved it.

Do not allow your budget to dictate how meaningful your celebration can be. A quiet, creatively focused evening alone with your spouse can result in a lifelong memory. If you're single, celebrate with a close friend or two. Celebrate whenever you can, even the small victories. For example, you may have a half dozen credit card debts. Celebrate each time you pay one off.

As you progress on your Money Map journey, arriving at Destination 4, then 5, 6, and 7, you will discover that each new destination enables you to afford to spend a little more on your celebrations.

During the celebration, I suggest doing something that will remind you of your progress. When you pay off a credit card debt, you might burn a copy of the last statement. Frame the first dollar you save toward the $1,000 emergency savings fund for Destination 1. Be creative and have fun! Let your joy become a contagious motivator.

Donnie and Peggy Moore invited a group of friends to join them when they celebrated paying off their home by burning their mortgage. Tom and Donna Keebler attended and were amazed at the thought of having a home free and clear. They caught the vision and started adding extra money to their payment each month, accelerating their own debt-free, mortgage-free day—all because a friend asked them to attend a celebration.

Roadside Assistance—Online!

Identify what you would like to do or have as you celebrate reaching your destinations on the Crown Money Map. Visit the **CrownMoneyMap.org** to learn about creative celebration ideas. Then pray about it. Talk about it. And go for it! Later, return to the Web site to tell others about your creative celebration.

*"Unless you assume a god, the question
of life's purpose is meaningless."*

— BERTRAND RUSSELL

atheist

*"You were made by God and for God—and until you
understand that, life will never make any sense."*

— RICK WARREN

Christian

WHAT ON EARTH AM I HERE FOR?

"Over the weekend we learned more about each other than we could have possibly imagined," Matt reported.

"Yes, it definitely helped our marriage," Jennifer agreed enthusiastically. "We'd never really taken the time to talk about our dreams and goals. It was a huge breakthrough in our relationship."

I had given them an assignment: the next step in preparation for the journey to *true financial freedom*. They needed to begin to identify their life purposes and then set long-term and short-term goals to help them achieve those purposes.

Matt and Jennifer had gone to a friend's cabin in the nearby mountains. Free from distractions, they prayed and talked about what they sensed God wanted them to accomplish.

"What was your biggest surprise?" Bev asked.

"That's easy!" Jennifer laughed. "Matt thinks the Lord wants him to own a car dealership someday."

"It's true," Matt said, obviously embarrassed. "I know it's probably impossible, but I'd really like to have one and dedicate it to the Lord."

I smiled and put my arm around him. "Matt, it's not impossible. With the Lord's help you can do it. Remember, the Bible says, *'With God all things are possible.'*[1] And, Matt, this is one reason that following the Money Map is so beneficial. Every time you arrive at another destination, you'll be closer to the goal of owning a dealership.

HeyHoward@Crown.org

QUESTION: *Why is it important to write down my financial goals?*
ANSWER: *Writing down your goals is powerful because it helps you clarify your thinking, monitor your progress, and make mid-course corrections.*

"Now the reason it's important to identify what God wants you to accomplish is that it helps you focus; it actually simplifies your life. All of us have limited time and money. Once we understand our purpose, we can use both of them more effectively."

"But I really don't know my purpose," Jennifer interrupted. "Of course, I want to do a good job of raising our children. And I'd like to help families adopt children, because I'm adopted."

"I didn't realize you were adopted!" Bev exclaimed. "That's so neat! Well, anyway, you two are further along than we were when we started out. Howard had an interest in helping people learn God's way of handling money, and I knew that our children were going to be my primary focus for a while. That's about all we knew at the time."

"That's right," I affirmed. "Even though we didn't fully understand our life purposes, we decided to *prepare* ourselves to be financially free for whatever the Lord would reveal to us in the future."

GOD HAS A PURPOSE FOR YOU.

God intends for each of us to fulfill a special purpose. The Bible says this about King David, *"For when David had served **God's** purpose in his own generation . . . [he died and] was buried."*[2]

Did you notice that David served *God's* purpose? This is important to realize: It's not about what *you* want to do with your life, it's about what *God* wants to do with it. Look at what God told Jeremiah. *"Before I formed you in the womb I knew you, before you were born I set you apart; I appointed you* [for a task]*."*[3]

God has a particular purpose in mind for you. The Bible says, *"We are God's workmanship, created in Christ Jesus to do good works, which God prepared in advance for us to do."*[4] Let's look at this passage. "We are God's workmanship." Another translation says, *"We are God's own handiwork."*[5]

Just as God gave you unique fingerprints, you have been created like no one else in human history. He custom-made you for a special task, and He gave you just the right personality, abilities, and desires to accomplish this work. The Bible says, *"God has given each of us the ability to do certain things well."*[6]

> *You have been created like no one else in human history. God custom-made you for a special task, and He gave you just the right personality, abilities, and desires to accomplish this work.*

Most of us struggle with too many things to do and too little time in which to do them. The good can become the enemy of the best. Once we understand the role God has for us, it becomes easier to evaluate opportunities and decline those that distract us from achieving our purpose.

I have two close friends. One has average ability, but he has been remarkably successful because he has been single-minded. The other is much more gifted, but he scattered his energies by pursuing too many projects with limited success. Knowing your purpose helps you become more productive.

IDENTIFY YOUR PURPOSE.

Consider three steps to help you recognize your purpose. The first one is to pray. Just as the best way to discover a machine's purpose is to ask its manufacturer, you can ask your Creator to reveal your purpose.

> *"The thing is to understand myself, to see what God really wishes me to do . . . to find the idea for which I can live and die."*
>
> SØREN KIERKEGAARD

The second step is to read the Bible regularly. The Bible makes this remarkable claim about itself: *"The word of God is living and active. Sharper than any double-edged sword . . . it judges the thoughts and attitudes of the heart."* [7] I have found this to be true. God used a particular verse from the Bible to clarify my purpose. The Bible is a living book that God uses to communicate His direction and truths.

The third step is to experiment with different areas of service. God often reveals our purpose as we serve. That's how the Lord later confirmed my purpose. I was thoroughly enjoying leading a Crown small group financial study when it suddenly dawned on me: this is what God made me for!

Many people get the discovery process backwards. They say, "Discover your purpose and then you'll know in what capacity to serve." It usually works in the opposite way. Just start serving, and then trust God to reveal your purpose.

As you seek to identify your purpose, keep in mind that *your purpose may be large . . . or it may be small.* Some roles are visible and some are behind the scenes. Some are large and some are small, but in God's sight all are *equally* valuable. There is no correlation between size and significance. For example, think of the enormous impact parents can have by quietly investing time in nurturing their child, or the profound influence of teachers on a few students. Every task is important.

If God subtracted one pain, one heartache, one disappointment from my life, I would be less than the person I am now, less the person God wants me to be, and my ministry would be less than He intends."

RON DUNN

Also keep in mind that *sometimes God prepares you through difficulties.* What painful experiences have you endured? God never wastes a difficult circumstance. Who is better able to help a divorced person than one who has been through a hurtful divorce and recovered well? Who can better help a drug user or an alcoholic than someone who has overcome these addictions?

The Bible says it this way: *"God . . . so wonderfully comforts and strengthens us in our hardships and trials. And why does he do this? So that when others are troubled, needing our sympathy and encouragement, we can pass on to them the same help and comfort God has given us."* [8]

BEGIN THE PROCESS.

As you begin the process, it may be a helpful example for me to share my own purposes with you. Eventually I sensed God has three purposes for me:

1. To influence my family and friends to know Jesus Christ as their Savior and to grow close to Him.
2. To teach as many people as possible God's financial principles.
3. To leave the legacy of practical financial materials based on the Bible.

Now it's your turn to begin identifying your purpose. I want to encourage you not to rush though this process. Remember, understanding what God wants you to do with your life will have an enormous influence on how you choose to spend money. So pray. Take your time. Consider this carefully.

To help you begin, consider your purpose in these areas and do your best to describe it.

My relationship with God _____

_____

_____

_____

My relationship with family and friends _____

_____

_____

_____

My service to others _____

_____

_____

Then, to the best of your understanding, answer these questions.

What do I believe God created me to be and do? _____

_____

_____

_____

How would I summarize my life purpose? _____

_____

_____

_____

What Bible verse communicates my life purpose? _____

_____

_____

_____

You may not have been able to answer these questions completely, but now you have the framework that will help you discover your purpose. If you are married, answer these questions individually and then discuss them with your spouse.

WRITE YOUR GOALS.

Once you begin to identify your life purpose, establish long-term and short-term goals. These are achievable steps that will help you reach your life purpose.

For instance, if you are a single parent and you want to help fund your children's college, consider the steps you will need to take. These become your goals. Your long-term goal would be to have a certain amount of savings for their education. Short-term goals might include paying off debts, increasing your income, perhaps even downsizing to more affordable housing.

Or perhaps you are a working wife and you want to have children someday and stay home to raise them. Similarly, consider the steps you will need to take. These become your goals. One of your long-term goals would be to make ends meet on just your husband's income.

It is smart to first establish your long-term goals, and then identify your shorter-term goals as intermediate steps. For example, if you know your ten-year goals, it will be easier for you to determine the goals you will need to accomplish in five years, in three years, and this year.

Writing down your goals is a powerful but often neglected step that helps you clarify and prioritize them. The mystery fades as you monitor your progress and make midcourse corrections. Written goals create momentum, helping you focus on the priorities that will enable you to achieve your purpose.

As you work on your goals, remember that money is not the goal; it is simply a *tool*—one that will help you accomplish the goals that will fulfill your life purpose.

IDENTIFYING YOUR GOALS

With that in mind, begin by identifying your goals. Write down your long-term goals for each of the areas that follow.

Long-Term Goals

Relationship with God: _____

_____

Family and friends: _____

_____

Service to others: _____

_____

Career/Skills/Education: _____

_____

Long-Term Financial Goals

*Giving:*_____

_____

*Spending/Lifestyle:*_____

_____

Saving and investing: _____

_____

*Debt:*_____

_____

*Other:*_____

_____

Short-Term Goals

Once you have established your long-term goals, work backwards and write down what you want to achieve over the short-term, including this year. A word of caution: Don't be discouraged if you are not successful in accomplishing all of the goals you've set for a particular year. I rarely reach all of mine. However, when you know your goals, you know what you want to get done. You have a target. With God's help, you can make progress.

Relationship with God: _____

_____

Family and friends: _____

_____

Service to others: _____

_____

Career/Skills/Education: _____

_____

Short-Term Financial Goals

*Giving:*_____

_____

*Spending/Lifestyle:*_____

_____

Saving and Investing: _____

_____

*Debt:*_____

_____

*Other:*_____

_____

Roadside Assistance—Online!

Trip Log. You can complete and save your "Life Purpose" and "Life Goals" online in the Trip Log at **CrownMoneyMap.org**.

Diligence is the mother of good fortune.

—CERVANTES

Whatever you do, do your work heartily,
as for the Lord rather than for men.

—THE APOSTLE PAUL

MAKING THE
MOST
OUT OF YOUR JOB

On the way to work my cell phone rang. It was Matt Mitchell. He knew I was scheduled to bring my car in for service. "When you come in today, could we talk?" he asked.

"Sure, Matt. What's up?" I asked

"I've been thinking about something you said a while back—that with God's help it might be possible to own a car dealership someday. It's what I'd really like to do. I love the business, and think I could make a go of it."

After leaving the car for service, I met with Matt, and he got right to the point. "You've started businesses before. What are some of the things I should do to prepare myself?"

"Well, there's a big difference between being a good salesman and operating a dealership," I responded. "You've got to learn the business from top to bottom; from the sales department to the service department.

"I know you respect the owner of the dealership. I'd encourage you to ask him to take you on as a management trainee."

"That's a great idea," Matt said. "Mr. Johnson grew up in the business.

I'll ask him. What do I have to lose?

"Jennifer and I also realize that if we want to accelerate our journey to true financial freedom," Matt continued, "we need to increase our income somehow. Even a little would make a big difference."

Matt was right; a little increase can make a *big* difference. During a career, the average person works more than 100,000 hours. Do the math: Earning $2.50 more per hour adds up to $250,000. An additional $5.00 per hour equals $500,000 more over a lifetime.

WHAT GOD SAYS ABOUT WORK

The key that unlocks the door to earning more is understanding what the Bible says about work. The first thing God did with Adam was to put him to work. *"The LORD God took the man and put him in the Garden of Eden to work it and take care of it. "*[1] God instituted work for *our* benefit in the sinless environment of the garden of Eden. Work is so important that God gave this command: *"You shall work six days. "*[2] The apostle Paul added, *"If anyone is not willing to work, then he is not to eat, either. "*[3]

Work develops our character.

One of the primary purposes of work is to develop *us*. While the carpenter is building a house, the house is also building the carpenter. His skill, diligence, manual dexterity, and judgment are refined. A job is not merely a task designed to earn money; it's also intended to produce godly character in the life of the worker.

A close friend has a brother in his mid-forties whose parents have always supported him. He has never faced the responsibilities and hardships involved in a job. As a consequence, his character has not been developed and he is hopelessly immature.

All honest professions are honorable.

The Bible does not elevate any honest profession above another. David was a shepherd and a king. Luke was a doctor. Lydia was a retailer. Daniel was a government worker. Paul was a tentmaker, and Jesus was a carpenter. Regardless of what our culture thinks of your job, God views it as valuable as any other honest job.

GOD'S ROLE IN OUR WORK

God is actively involved in our work, and He has several important responsibilities.

God gives job skills.

The Bible says that to *"every skilled person . . . to whom **the LORD** has given skill and ability to know how to carry out all the work."*[4] God has given each of us job skills. People have a wide variety of abilities, manual skills, and intellectual capacities. It is not a matter of one person being better than another; it is simply a matter of having received different abilities.

> *One of the primary purposes of work is to develop us. A job is not merely a task designed to earn money; it's also intended to produce godly character in the life of the worker.*

God controls promotion and success.

As much as it may surprise you, your boss is not the one who controls whether you will be promoted. The Bible says, *"For promotion and power come from nowhere on earth, but only from God."*[5] The Bible also reveals the reason for Joseph's success: *"The LORD was with Joseph and he prospered . . . the LORD gave him success in everything he did."*[6] What was true for Joseph is true for us.

Most people leave God completely out of their work. They believe they alone control their success and promotions and are solely responsible for their job skills. However, those with a biblical understanding approach work knowing God is personally involved in it.

One of the major reasons people experience frustration in their jobs is that they don't understand God's role. Answer this: How will knowing the part God plays in your work impact you and your job?

OUR RESPONSIBILITIES IN WORK

Throughout the Bible, hard work is encouraged. *"Whatever your hand finds to do, do it with all your might."*[7] *"The precious possession of a man is diligence."*[8] Laziness, on the other hand, is condemned: *"He also who is slack in his work is brother to him who destroys."*[9]

FRANK'S NOT WHAT YOU'D CALL A MORNING PERSON.

© *Mark Sisson. Used by permission.*

Hard work, however, must be *balanced* by rest and the other priorities of life. The Bible says, *"You shall work six days, but on the seventh day you shall rest; even during plowing time and harvest you shall rest."*[10] If your job requires so much of your time and energy that you neglect your relationship with Christ or your loved ones, then you are working too much.

Rest can be an issue of faith. Is God able to make our six days of work more productive than seven days? Yes! He instituted rest for our physical, mental, and spiritual health.

STARTLING STATS:

Americans have widespread dissatisfaction with their jobs. The average man changes jobs every four and one-half years, the average woman every three years.

Just who is your boss?

The Bible says we are actually serving God in our work, not just people. *"Whatever you do, do your work heartily, as for the Lord rather than for men. . . . It is the Lord Christ whom you serve."*[11] Recognizing that we are working for the Lord Himself has profound implications. Consider your attitude. If you could see Jesus Christ as your boss, would you try to work harder and perform at a higher level? Would you be more committed to excellence in your job? When we "work heartily, as for the Lord," our job performance improves, which often translates into earning more money.

FINDING THE RIGHT JOB

Finding the right vocation is huge. If you are in a job for which God gave you an aptitude coupled with desire, you will look forward to work. It will feel more like a *vacation* than a *vocation*. Finding the perfect vocation can be the difference between job satisfaction or dissatisfaction, the difference between earning adequate or inadequate income. If you are unemployed or in a career for which you are not well suited, the first step is to discover the right job.

Aptitude Testing

I recommend career-related aptitude testing to help you narrow your focus. There are many assessments available, and some are quite expensive. You can log on the Money Map Web site to learn about the *Career Direct Complete Guidance System*, an outstanding personal growth resource that was developed over a ten-year period and is fully validated for accuracy. It is reasonably priced and more than 120,000 individuals have benefited from it.[12] *Career Direct* assesses your personality, interests, skills, and values to help

you identify your best potential careers. *Career Direct* may be completed online. Enter your password (found in the back of this book on the *Career Direct* information page) to receive a discount.

"Here's a tip. The next time you send out a hundred resumés, don't send them all to the same company."

© *David Cooney. Used by permission.*

Once you have decided on the career you want to pursue, prepare yourself by acquiring the necessary job skills, education, and experience.

Next Steps

When you begin searching for a job, complete an accurate resume of your experiences that would be important for a potential employer to know. Then take these steps:

- Pray for God to provide you with just the right job opportunities.
- Research potential jobs.
- Beat the bushes—network with as many people as possible, telling them of the job you are seeking.

TRANSITIONING FROM JOBS

When you are moving from one job to another, it is important to be absolutely faithful to your *current* employer until you leave. Too many people slack off in their work, and some even sow seeds of discord during their transition. However, when you work hard to the end and leave well, you are more likely to experience God's blessing in your new job.

HeyHoward@Crown.org

QUESTION: *I've been using a budget and don't spend one cent on anything that is not an absolute need, but I'm still not able to make ends meet. What should I do?*

ANSWER: *You're simply not earning enough money. You need to find a job for which you are well-suited that will produce more income. I'd start by taking an aptitude test to identify your best potential careers. Then pray and network like crazy to find the right job.*

WHEN YOU ARE ALREADY IN THE RIGHT JOB

If you are currently working in a job that is perfect for you, you can do several things to position yourself to earn more money.

Be a lifelong learner.

Continually seek to improve your job performance. If you could become more useful to your employer by learning computer skills, take a course to become computer proficient. The more you develop your competencies, the more valuable you become and the more your employer will be willing to pay you.

Honor your boss.

This crucial principle is often violated. Godly employees should always honor their superiors. The Bible says,

"[Employees], *submit yourselves to your* [employer] *with all respect, not only to those who are good and considerate, but also to those who are harsh.*"[13]

Linda worked for a terribly demanding and difficult boss in a large aerospace company. She decided, however, to do everything she could to help him succeed. If he was scheduled to make a presentation to upper management, she worked long hours to produce the very best one. She was loyal, never participating in office gossip behind his back. In short, she was faithful.

When the company lost several large government contracts, it was forced to lay off thousands of employees. Linda was scheduled to lose her job. Quietly, her boss talked to other department heads and told them of Linda's excellent performance. Instead of losing her job, she was transferred to another department and given a 30 percent raise! Faithfulness puts us in a position to experience God's blessing.

Godly employees always honor their superiors.

Earning More Income

Some jobs simply do not produce enough income to make progress on the Money Map. My son, Matthew, has such a job. He serves as the children's director of the Orlando Rescue Mission, and he *loves* it! This is what God prepared Matthew to do. About sixty homeless children live at the mission, and he has an incredible opportunity to influence them positively for the rest of their lives. Because of Matthew's commitment to these children, he has turned down higher paying jobs. He had to figure out a creative way to supplement his salary so he and his wife could move forward on their financial journey.

CHECKING OUT THE SECOND INCOME

The two-income family is the norm today, with both husband and wife assuming they must work outside the home to make ends meet. Their assumption may not be correct.

Couples are often surprised to learn that after deducting taxes and expenses, the income earned by a second working spouse is not as much as they had expected. Some have actually produced more net income when they decided to work from home rather than outside of the home.

Denise and her husband sought the help of one of Crown's volunteer Money Map coaches. Denise was working forty hours a week and earning $9.35 an hour. After they reviewed all her taxes, payroll deductions, and expenses for the year, here is what they discovered.

	Denise	*Your Situation*
Income:	$ 18,720	_____
Expenses:		
Giving	$1,872	_____
Taxes & payroll deductions	6,500	_____
Additional transportation	1,300	_____
Lunch & coffee breaks	500	_____
Extra eating out	600	_____
Extra clothing/cleaning	800	_____
Personal grooming	360	_____
Day care 2 kids @ $55 ea/wk	5,500	_____
Total expenses:	$17,432	_____
Real Net Income:	$1,288	_____
Net income per hour:	$.64	_____

Your situation may be dramatically different from Denise's, but I encourage you to check it out. Remember, you need to know the facts before you can make informed decisions.

WORKING FROM HOME

More people are working from home these days—stay-at-home parents, the disabled, retirees, and those caring for adults or children with special needs. Many jobs lend themselves to working out of the home, such as child care, bookkeeping, and small businesses. Advances in technology mean that just about anyone with a phone and a computer has more opportunities to work in the home.

I mentioned this to Matt, and he recognized the potential.

"That's something Jennifer could do," Matt said. "She's very talented and for some time has wanted to do a little work from home to earn some extra money."

"Well, encourage her to pursue this," I responded. "Remember, a little additional income can often make a big difference on your journey to *true financial freedom.*"

Roadside Assistance—Online!

Use the How Much Do You Really Make? calculator at the **CrownMoney Map.org** Web site to determine the net income of the second wage earner in your household.

2 MAKING PROGRESS ON THE JOURNEY

I joined a Crown small group study in late 2000 because I hoped it would teach me about investing. Three years earlier I had launched a recruiting firm to help companies find talent in the information technology (IT) field. In two years my salary tripled to the six-figure range, which was a major feat for a single mom raising a son.

But during the Crown class, God showed me that I was not giving sacrificially. He began opening opportunities for me to give sacrificially to other people, and I did. Unfortunately, what I didn't do was make a plan to get out of debt. Instead, I increased my standard of living.

I never would have expected during these good times that the IT market would crash, but it did. My annual salary dropped from six figures to $20,000. My car and house were repossessed, and I even had to seek charity to help me pay rent.

Creditors knocked on my door and called me at home and at work. In turn, I cried out to God, who showed me I hadn't been completely faithful in handling all my money.

I let go of my pride and became transparent about my situation. My car was returned to me, and even though I didn't get my house back, it didn't go down on my credit report. I'm now the Crown coordinator at my church, and we've launched twelve groups this semester.

Currently, I'm at Destination 3 on the Money Map, with only one consumer debt to repay. Through the lessons I learned, my son, now twenty-three, chose to follow God's financial principles. He has purchased his first house and has a plan to pay it off in seven years.

— **HELEN NELSON,** *Atlanta, Georgia*

*Read and watch more stories along the journey at **CrownMoneyMap.org**.*

PART 2 DISCUSSION QUESTIONS

1. Do you consistently give generously and from a heart of love? Why or why not?

2. Are you honest in even the smallest matters? If not, what will you do to become a person of integrity?

3. What will you do to celebrate the first time you make progress on your journey to true financial freedom? With whom will you celebrate?

4. Try to describe what you believe to be your life purpose.

5. What one-year and five-year goals will you establish to help you accomplish your life purpose?

6. Have you discovered what career you are designed and best suited to pursue? Are you working in that career now? If not, what will you do to prepare for it?

PART 2 TOOLS FOR YOUR JOURNEY

Tools to Help with Your Giving

- *The Treasure Principle,* by Randy Alcorn (Sisters, OR: Multnomah, 2005).

- *The Treasure Principle,* DVD and workbook, is an effective way for groups and classes to learn the joy of giving. Crown Financial Ministries.

- *Generous Giving* is an organization that has a superb Web site and materials to help people become well informed, joyful givers. Go to www.Generous Giving.org for more information.

- *National Christian Foundation* is an excellent donor-advised fund. Go to www.NationalChristian.com for more information.

Tool to Help in Identifying Your Purpose and Goals

The Purpose Driven Life, by Rick Warren (Grand Rapids: Zondervan 2002).

Tool to Help in Your Job and Career

People who enjoy their work are far more likely to succeed. Maximize your effectiveness in life and work with the *Career Direct Complete Guidance System.* As a special offer to people like you on the journey to true financial freedom, a discount code is in the back of this book.

PART

3

DESTINATIONS 1 and *2*

Debt is bad, saving is good, giving is fun,
and stuff is meaningless.

— ANGELA CORRELL
Author

CHAPTER 11

DESTINATION 1:
SAVING FOR
EMERGENCIES

"Well, are you ready to buckle up and start the journey to true financial freedom?" I asked Matt and Jennifer. I unfolded the Crown Money Map and continued. "Let's review what you've done to prepare for the trip. First, you learned the basics of what the Bible says about handling money. Then you began to identify your life purposes and established goals that will help you achieve your purposes. And you've also made some career decisions that could increase your income."

"And for the past thirty days we've kept track of every penny we've spent," Matt interjected.

"And don't forget the financial statement," Jennifer added. "Now we know exactly what we own and how much we owe."

"That's right," Bev responded. "You've made real progress as you've packed your bags for the journey."

"Now, on to Destination 1," I said, smiling. "There are two objectives for Destination 1. First, you'll save $1,000 for emergencies, and second, you'll start using a spending plan."

Matt and Jennifer groaned in unison. Then in a voice barely above a whisper, Matt said, "We've never been able to save regularly because of our spending habits."

"That's not unusual," I said. "But there's a good reason for saving, and it helps if you understand it. We want you to save $1,000 for emergencies because they are inevitable. Tires go flat, refrigerators go on the fritz—the list is endless.

"There are several things you should know about the emergency savings. First, it is set aside for *emergencies only*. It should be quickly accessible, so put it in something that will earn interest but you can get your hands on immediately. A money market fund with check writing privileges would be a good choice. Don't let your retirement savings or investments double as emergency savings.

THE SAVING SLOPE

Unfortunately, most people are not consistent savers. The average person in our country is three weeks away from bankruptcy. Most have significant debt, little or no money saved, and depend on the next paycheck to make ends meet. Look at the graph below. It's shocking! Americans saved an average of 10.8 percent of their income in 1984. By 2005, their rate of saving had fallen to a *negative* .5 percent, the lowest savings rate in the past seventy-three years!

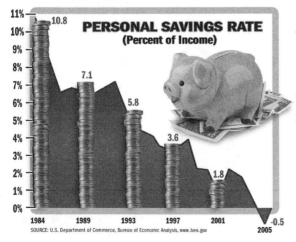

PERSONAL SAVINGS RATE
(Percent of Income)

SOURCE: U.S. Department of Commerce, Bureau of Economic Analysis, www.bea.gov

The Bible, on the other hand, encourages us to save: *"The wise man saves for the future, but the foolish man spends whatever he gets."* [1] God commends the ant for saving for a future need. *"Four things on earth are small, yet they are extremely wise: ants are creatures of little strength, yet they store up their food in the summer."* [2]

We all need to think like the

"extremely wise" ant when it comes to saving. Even though ants are small, they save. You may not be in a position to save a lot right now, but beginning the habit even in a small way is always smart.

The Bible tells us that Joseph saved during *"seven years of great abundance"*[3] in order to survive during *"seven years of famine."*[4] That is the essence of saving: putting the brakes on spending today so that you will have something to spend in the future. Most people are poor savers because they don't see the value in practicing self-denial. Our culture screams that we deserve to get what we want, when we want it! We can always pay later.

AMATEURS VERSUS THE PROS

Controlling spending is especially hard because we live in the biggest consumer society in all history. Why are billions of advertising dollars spent every day? There is only one reason—they want our money! Everywhere we turn, someone is pitching their stuff. Television, radio, the Internet, billboards, newspapers, magazines, shopping malls—the list goes on and on. Every day exposes us to a new flood of messages to buy something.

Advertisers have become incredibly sophisticated in their techniques to induce us to spend. They invest millions on surveys and testing to determine the most effective ways to hook us into buying. They spend a fortune choosing the best name, the best colors, and the most emotionally powerful images to market their products.

When we try to beat them at their own game, it is impossible to win. It's the amateurs versus the pros, and guess who the amateurs are? We are! The only way we can win is to ask God to give us the mind-set that says, "Nothing I buy feels as good as reaching *true financial freedom.*"

HOW TO RESIST THE CALLS TO SPEND AND SPEND

There are three practical things you can do to stand against this relentless onslaught of advertising to spend and spend.

1. Limit your exposure.

It seems almost un-American in this "Shop 'til you drop" society, but one of the most effective ways to bring spending under control is to intentionally isolate yourself from the temptations to spend. Consider this:

STARTLING STATS:

Eighty-two percent of middle-income Americans say there is not much money left to save after they have paid their bills.

- The more television you watch, the more you spend.
- The more you surf the Web, the more you spend.
- The more you look at catalogues and magazines, the more you spend.
- The more you shop, the more you spend.

When my daughter was younger, I could tell when she had watched television. Suddenly, she just had to have a certain toy. If she hadn't seen the commercial, she would have been perfectly content without it. Here is the simple truth: Limiting your exposure to spending opportunities helps you control your spending.

2. Cultivate Contentment

Advertisers frequently try to create discontentment with what we have. Our consumption-oriented society operates on the assumption that happiness comes from things, and more is always better. That's why keeping up with the Joneses has become a national pastime. The result is widespread discontent. In contrast, God wants you to be content. Contentment is mentioned seven times in Scripture, and six times it has to do with money.

If you cannot be content with what you have, you will never be content with what you want.

The apostle Paul wrote, *"I have learned to be content whatever the circumstances. I know what it is to be in need, and I know what it is to have plenty. I have learned the secret of being content in any and every situation, whether well fed or hungry, whether living in plenty or in want. I can do everything through him who gives me strength.*"[5] Paul learned to be content. No one is born with the instinct of contentment; rather, we must learn it.

Contentment enables us to live within our means. It values the true riches of relationships with God, family, and friends. It resists the urge to buy, buy, buy!

3. Pray for God to provide.

When Bev and I first determined to work toward true financial freedom, we decided that we would pray and wait for the Lord to provide things rather than rush to buy them.

As we walk around our home, we are overwhelmed with items that He has provided. There was the gift of our dining room table and chairs, the $3 solid-oak chair from a garage sale, and the headboard for our bed—for which we waited ten years.

Most of the furnishings in our home have a story that is a tangible reminder of God's love and provision.

IT STARTS IN THE MIND

Once when Bev and Jennifer got together, my wife confided how she had struggled with her weight for more than fifteen years, finally losing more than fifty pounds

"How much?" Jennifer asked in amazement. "How did you do it? Did you go on a radical diet or something?"

"No," Bev explained, admitting she'd tried dozens of diets with no lasting success. "Finally, I simply decided on a healthy way of eating."

"Then I looked at what the Bible says about our bodies. It says, *'Don't you know that you yourselves are God's temple and that God's Spirit lives in you? If anyone destroys God's temple, God will destroy him; for God's temple is sacred, and you are that temple.'*[6] I meditated on this passage and came to understand that the Lord lives in my body and that I need to be faithful to take care of it.

"I prayed that God would give me the mental discipline to eat wisely for both weight loss and overall health. Next, I established a goal for how much I wanted to lose. Then I joined a gym and started to work out regularly to burn more calories. And it definitely helped when Howard agreed to eat the same way.

"I weighed myself once a week to gauge progress, knowing that some weeks I would lose and other weeks I'd gain a little. I stayed encouraged by reading helpful books, and I even led a class for those who wanted to lose weight.

"I also memorized several Bible verses and a few jingles that I'd recite whenever I was tempted to eat something I shouldn't."

As Bev told her story, it brought back all kinds of memories. "I've heard those jingles so often I can repeat them: 'Nothing tastes as good as slim feels.' 'Ten seconds on the lips means ten pounds on the hips.' 'If you don't need it, don't eat it.'"

The True Financial Freedom Mind-set

There are lessons from Bev's weight loss that will help you reach *true financial freedom.*

First, *meditate.* Select several passages from the Bible that deal with God's perspective on handling money. For saving, this is a good choice: *"The wise man saves for the future, but the foolish man spends whatever he gets."*[7] For getting out of debt, memorize, *"The borrower is servant to the lender."*[8] Meditate on them. Let them produce in you a passion to apply the principles.

> *God wants to be involved in every area of your life. He desires for you to know Him well and discover how deeply He loves you.*

Second, *pray.* Ask the Lord to give you the necessary discipline and persistence to reach your next destination on the Money Map. Some people are reluctant to pray for God's help with their finances.

The Bible says, *"Do not be anxious about anything, but in **everything**, by prayer and petition, with thanksgiving, present your requests to God"*[9] Did you see that? You're to pray about everything. God wants to be involved in every area of your life. He desires for you to know Him well and discover how deeply He loves you. In the journey to true financial freedom, nothing is more important than asking for His assistance.

Third, *Focus on the next destination and go for it!*

What Bev did to reach her destination you can do:.

- *Look at the facts.* She stepped on the scales once a week to monitor her progress. The scales told her the truth about how well she was doing. This is the reason it is important to keep your spending plan current and review it regularly.

- *Accelerate the goal.* Bev started exercising at the gym to lose weight more rapidly. If you can earn even a little more money, it is amazing how much faster you will reach your destinations.

- *Involve your spouse.* If you are married, it makes all the difference when you and your spouse work together. The Bible says, *"If a house is divided against itself, that house cannot stand."*[10] Meet together regularly to pray, review the facts, discuss how to improve, and celebrate the victories.

> **HeyHoward@Crown.org**
>
> **QUESTION:** *How often should my husband and I review our spending plan?*
>
> **ANSWER:** *Meet at least once a week to pray, review your financial progress, and celebrate the victories. Use this as an opportunity to grow closer together as a couple.*

Overcoming Discouragement and Temptation

The journey to true financial freedom is not easy. At times you may want to quit. Bev faced a similar challenge while trying to lose weight because she *loves* chocolate. But she realized that if she gave in to her desires, her dream of losing weight would remain just that—a dream. The battle was in her mind.

That is when she would remind herself, "Nothing tastes as good as slim feels." "Ten seconds on the lips means ten pounds on the hips." "If I don't need it, I won't eat it."

I want you to write these down (or create your own) and carry them with you:

Nothing I buy feels as good as reaching true financial freedom.

Ten seconds using my credit card, ten months to pay it off.

If I don't need it, I won't buy it.

Much of the battle to reach your next destination takes place in your mind. You need to remind yourself constantly of the goal. It has to become more important to you than spending money on things you really don't need.

> *If you **immediately** save a portion of every paycheck, you will save more.*

PRACTICAL SUGGESTIONS FOR SAVING

The most effective way to save is to make it automatic. When you receive income, the first check you write should be a gift to the Lord, and the second check should go to savings. An automatic payroll deduction can ensure that you regularly save some of your income. Some people save their tax refunds or bonuses. Remember this: if you *immediately* save a portion of every paycheck, you will save more.

The Bible does not teach an amount or percentage to be saved. We recommend saving 10 percent of your income. This may not be possible initially. But begin the habit of saving—even if it's only a dollar a month.

"People buy things they don't need with money they don't have to impress people they don't even like."
— GEORGE FOOSHEE
Author

If your outgo exceeds your income, your upkeep will be your downfall.
— ANONYMOUS

CHAPTER 12

DESTINATION 1:
YOUR
SPENDING
PLAN

Jennifer's eyes were red and Matt's face was the picture of discouragement.

"Tell us what happened," Bev ventured.

"We feel like we got buried by an avalanche," Matt said. "It's been one thing after another this month. One of our credit card companies hiked our interest rates to something like 20 percent. And my sales this month have been way off, so the commissions I expected just won't be there."

"It's even worse than that," Jennifer said in near panic. "It's not just this month. We're spending about $500 more than we make *every* month! No wonder we're in trouble!"

"We were so encouraged when we were with you last time," she continued. "But it feels like we're haunted by our past financial mistakes. I don't know what we're going to do. We can't pay all the bills. We feel like we're drowning . . . and giving seems to be out of the question."

"When we last met," I reassured them, "I remember warning you that you might be frustrated by what the spending plan reveals. Most people have

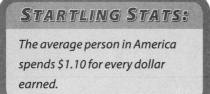

no idea that the average person in our country spends $1.10 for every dollar earned. The first draft of a spending plan usually has more outgo than income. *But take heart— there's hope!* I believe you can make adjustments and balance it. Let's take a look at your spending plan."

After a brief review, I said, "Hmmm, I think I can see some areas where you can cut expenses. However, I've learned that it's also important to give generously. It's counterintuitive, and I know it's a real stretch for you, but generosity is one of the keys to progress on the journey to *true financial freedom*."

DEVELOP YOUR SPENDING PLAN

I don't like to use the "B" word—budget—because so many people think of a budget as restrictive, a loss of freedom. They also fear it will require endless hours of monotonous, detailed accounting.

The term *spending plan* is more accurate. It suggests that you are telling your money where *you* want it to go rather than wondering where it went. A spending plan enables you to use your money to reach your goals and life purpose. It helps you control impulse spending, get out of debt, save consistently, and give generously. If you're not using a spending plan, chances are you are flying by the seat of your financial pants. You may be like the depositor who replied in disbelief to the banker, "What do you mean, I'm overdrawn? I still have six checks left in my checkbook!"

> *"Annual income twenty pounds, annual expenditure nineteen—result happiness. Annual income twenty pounds, annual expenditure twenty-one pounds—result misery."*
>
> CHARLES DICKENS

There are five steps you'll take to develop your spending plan.

Step 1: Record your income and spending for thirty days.

Just as Matt and Jennifer did, keep track of *every* penny spent and earned for thirty days to get an accurate picture of the facts. Then record all expenditures under the appropriate spending category—food, housing, clothing, etc. This prepares you for Step 2.

Step 2: Complete the first draft of your spending plan.

Based on what you learned in Step 1, estimate your monthly income and spending in each category of the spending plan on page 126.

Deciding what percentage of your income to allocate for each spending category can be difficult without any outside guidance. Log on to Crown MoneyMap.org to review national averages for successful spending plans.

Step 3: Adjust your spending plan.

If you are spending more than your income or if you want to accelerate your journey to *true financial freedom,* you must increase your income, reduce your expenses, or both. The objective is to create enough surplus in your spending plan to move toward your goals.

Ask yourself two questions about *every* expense: Do I really need this? Can I do this less expensively? Reducing spending means changing your lifestyle. This is never easy

Matt and Jennifer made hard decisions because of their commitment to reach *true financial freedom.* Compare their initial spending plan on page 124 with their adjusted one on page 125. The Mitchells' spending plan improved from a monthly deficit of $502 to a surplus of $210.

They made big cuts and small ones. Here's how they did it:

Spending reduced	*Monthly amount saved*
Cancel cable TV	$ 40
Use less electricity, water, phone	34
Sold car with highest loan	300
Less gas, car insurance, etc.	86
Less eating out and activities	85
Buy fewer clothes	70

Eliminate subscriptions	30
Less allowances and gifts	65
Enroll children in public school	<u>306</u>
Total Monthly Amount Saved	$1,016

They also decided to *increase* their giving to a full tithe—10 percent—from $200 to $490.

Step 4: Select your system.

Every spending plan employs one of four basic systems. Choose the one best suited for you.

1. *The envelope system.* Many of our grandparents used this; it still works! Label an envelope for each spending category. When the paycheck comes, divide the money according to plan and deposit it in the envelopes. When an envelope is empty, there is no more money to spend in that category.

2. *Pencil and paper.* Many people prefer using a standard checkbook and ledger system.

3. *PC-based budgeting software.* Many reasonably priced, user-friendly software programs are available to help you manage your personal finances.

4. *Web-based budgeting software.* A growing number of people are using powerful and secure budgeting systems connected to the Internet.

The key is to find a system you are comfortable using. For recommendations, visit CrownMoneyMap.org.

Step 5: Record and review.

Record your transactions and then review, review, review! Regularly review your spending plan because it is a dynamic tool that you will refine and alter over time. Your finances are not static. Purchasing a home, changing jobs, paying off debt, and increases in the cost of living will all change your spending plan.

HOW TO DEAL WITH AN UNPREDICTABLE INCOME

Some people who receive their income from self-employment or sales commissions or a sporadic work schedule argue that they can't use a spending plan because their income is unpredictable. Irregular income, however, simply magnifies the importance of using a spending plan.

If your income is inconsistent, estimate your yearly income and divide it by twelve to determine your average monthly income. Then work toward establishing a savings reserve from which you can draw steady income. For example, assume you are able to save $4,000 for this reserve, and your spending plan requires $3,000 income per month. If you earn $2,000 during a month, withdraw $1,000 from savings to meet your plan. If you earn $5,000 the next month, spend only the planned $3,000 and deposit the rest into the savings reserve.

As a salesperson on commission, Matt Mitchell was in this situation. I told him, "Matt, your biggest challenge will be during your high-income months, remembering not to spend everything you earn that month. Limit your spending to the planned amount so your reserve can be replenished."

SUGGESTIONS FOR YOUR SPENDING PLAN
Find a coach.

Many people discover that it's too difficult to start and sustain a spending plan without help. They need advice, encouragement, and accountability from someone who is using one successfully. We recommend that you ask someone experienced for assistance.

Compute variable expenses.

To establish an accurate spending plan, you need to account for spending that varies each month. These include utility bills, food, clothing, house and auto repairs, etc. Estimate the average monthly cost for each category by determining the annual amount and dividing by twelve.

HeyHoward@Crown.org

QUESTION: *I'm just not able to start a budget. Can you help me?*
ANSWER: *Many people need encouragement and accountability from someone who is using one successfully. Go to Crown MoneyMap.org for a trained volunteer who can help you in person or online.*

Become a team.

Husbands and wives should work *together* to develop their initial spending plan. This will require open, honest communication and usually some give-and-take. The Lord intended the husband and wife to be unified, which is why God said, "*A man shall . . . be joined to his wife; and they shall become one flesh.*"[1]

Once you have drawn up your initial spending plan, the spouse more gifted in keeping records should do the accounting. Then meet together once a week to examine your progress, discuss challenges, and make adjustments.

If you are a couple who wants the wife to stay home, design your spending plan based on only the husband's income. If the wife is working in advance of that, use her income for debt reduction and savings. The further you have progressed on your Money Map journey, the easier it will be to transition to being a stay-at-home mom.

Think annually.

When you evaluate an expense based on what it costs you for the year, it gives you a much better view of its true cost. If you eat lunch out every working day and spend an average of $6, it doesn't seem like much money. But this is $1,500 a year. A daily newspaper can add up to more than $300 a year, and visits to the coffee shop, $800. These "nickel and dime" expenditures can have a huge impact on your spending plan.

Get creative with holidays.

One of the biggest budget busters is excessive spending for Christmas, birthdays and other celebrations. Do not underestimate this; it is a real problem for many. A recent survey discovered that the biggest fear people have at Christmas time is Christmas debt! The bills that follow the spending binge send many people into depression. It doesn't have to be that way.

The key is establishing a strict budget—yes, I used the "B" word in this case! Your spending for gifts needs to be carefully controlled. Even people with average creativity—if they put their minds to it—can make or buy personalized gifts that are not expensive. The value of personalized gifts is their uniqueness and the way they reflect the recipient's interests.

Deal with gambling and compulsive spending.

If you have a problem with gambling or compulsive spending, it is crucial for you to admit it. You should not be embarrassed, because there are millions of people wrestling with the same thing. However, you do need help!

Become a member of a Christian support group. Address this issue for your financial and emotional health and for the sake of your loved ones.

Insurance

The image of the holidays is renewal and joy, but in reality for most Americans it's debt and exhaustion.

There are many types of insurance. Some of the most common are life, health, disability, homeowner's, automobile, liability, and business. In essence, insurance is a banding together of many people who each pay a small amount to protect the few who will actually experience a major expense due to illness, death, accident, or theft.

The amount and type of insurance you carry will be dictated by your *needs* and what you can *afford.* I address insurance in more detail in the appendix in the back of the book.

Remember, your spending plan is the practical tool that will help you accomplish your financial goals and life purpose. Visit CrownMoneyMap.org for more help with your spending plan.

MONTHLY SPENDING PLAN
Initial Draft
Matt and Jennifer Mitchell

Total Income	4,775		**5. Debts**	735
Salary	4,775		(except auto & house)	
Interest	25			
Dividends	25		**6. Entertainment/Recreation**	220
Other income			Eating out	120
Less			Babysitters	10
•Giving/Tithe	200		Activities/Trips	25
•Taxes	835		Vacation	50
			Pets	10
Spendable Income	3,864			
			7. Clothing	190
Living Expenses			**8. Savings**	0
1. Housing	1,385			
Mortgage or rent	1,030		**9. Medical**	40
Insurance	43		Doctor	20
Property taxes	60		Dentist	10
Electricity	92		Prescriptions	10
Cable TV	45		Other	0
Gas	12			
Water	8		**10. Miscellaneous**	219
Sanitation	10		Toiletries/Cosmetics	16
Telephone	35		Beauty/Barber	31
Maintenance	50		Laundry/Cleaning	12
Internet service	0		Allowances	70
Other	0		Subscriptions	30
			Gifts	60
2. Food	372		Other	0
3. Transportation	820		**11. School/Child Care**	316
Payments	575		Tuition	300
Gas & oil	55		Materials	16
Insurance	65		Transportation	0
License/Taxes	45		Day care	0
Auto maintenance	80			
Auto replacement	0		**12. Savings/Investments**	0
Other	0			
4. Insurance	73		*How the month turns out*	
Life	30		Spendable Income	3,864
Health/Dental	43		Minus Living Expenses	4,370
Disability	0		Monthly Surplus or Deficit	(506)
Other	0			

MONTHLY SPENDING PLAN
Adjusted Draft
Matt and Jennifer Mitchell

Total Income	4,775		**5. Debts**	735
Salary	4,775		(except auto & house)	
Interest	25			
Dividends	25		**6. Entertainment/Recreation**	135
Other income			Eating out	40
Less			Babysitters	10
•Giving/Tithe	490		Activities/Trips	20
•Taxes	761		Vacation	50
			Pets	15
Spendable Income	3,574			
			7. Clothing	120
Living Expenses			**8. Savings**	0
1. Housing	1,306			
Mortgage or rent	1,030		**9. Medical**	40
Insurance	43		Doctor	20
Property taxes	60		Dentist	10
Electricity	70		Prescriptions	10
Cable TV	0		Other	0
Gas	14			
Water	6		**10. Miscellaneous**	124
Sanitation	10		Toiletries/Cosmetics	16
Telephone	25		Beauty/Barber	31
Maintenance	40		Laundry/Cleaning	12
Internet service	0		Allowances	25
Other	0		Subscriptions	0
			Gifts	40
2. Food	372		Other	0
3. Transportation	449		**11. School/Child Care**	10
Payments	275		Tuition	0
Gas & oil	40		Materials	10
Insurance	40		Transportation	0
License/Taxes	25		Day care	0
Auto maintenance	54			
Auto replacement	0		**12. Savings/Investments**	0
Other	0			
4. Insurance	73		*How the month turns out*	
Life	30		Spendable Income	3,574
Health/Dental	43		Minus Living Expenses	3,364
Disability	0		Monthly Surplus or Deficit	210
Other	0			

SPENDING PLAN

Total Income _____
Salary _____
Interest _____
Dividends _____
Other income _____
Less
  •Giving/Tithe _____
  •Taxes _____

Spendable Income _____

Living Expenses
1. Housing _____
Mortgage or rent _____
Insurance _____
Property taxes _____
Electricity _____
Cable TV _____
Gas _____
Water _____
Sanitation _____
Telephone _____
Maintenance _____
Internet service _____
Other _____

2. Food _____

3. Transportation _____
Payments _____
Gas & oil _____
Insurance _____
License/Taxes _____
Auto maintenance _____
Auto replacement _____
Other _____

4. Insurance _____
Life _____
Health/Dental _____
Disability _____
Other _____

5. Debts _____
(except auto & house)

6. Entertainment/Recreation _____
Eating out _____
Babysitters _____
Activities/Trips _____
Vacation _____
Pets _____

7. Clothing _____

8. Savings _____

9. Medical _____
Doctor _____
Dentist _____
Prescriptions _____
Other _____

10. Miscellaneous _____
Toiletries/Cosmetics _____
Beauty/Barber _____
Laundry/Cleaning _____
Allowances _____
Subscriptions _____
Gifts _____
Other _____

11. School/Child Care _____
Tuition _____
Materials _____
Transportation _____
Day care _____

12. Savings/Investments _____

How the month turns out
Spendable Income _____
Minus Living Expenses _____
Monthly Surplus or Deficit _____

Roadside Assistance—Online!

If you need help starting your spending plan, ask a friend who is using one or visit **CrownMoneyMap.org** for a trained volunteer who can help you in person or online. This is a free service.

Electronic version of spending plan. For your convenience an electronic version of the spending plan is available on the Money Map Web site.

Crown's budgeting solutions. Learn more about Crown's four budgeting systems in the "Tools for Journey" section at the end of part 3 (page 141).

The borrower is servant to the lender.

— KING SOLOMON

Tenth century BC

[Be] free from the dominion of vice; by the practice of frugality, free from debt, which exposes a man to confinement and slavery to his creditors.

— BENJAMIN FRANKLIN

Eighteenth century AD

CHAPTER 13

DESTINATION 2:
CREDIT CARDS PAID OFF

The Mitchells asked Bev and me to meet them at their favorite ice-cream shop. There is nothing like a celebration, and reaching Destination 1 is a great reason to celebrate!

"We're so excited," Jennifer said over a chocolate ice-cream sundae. "I know we have a long way to go, but we're thankful that we have $1,000 saved for emergencies. And we are seeing the wisdom of using a spending plan for the first time in our lives."

"But, as you know, we've got a ton of credit card debt," Matt added as he took out the Crown Money Map. "We know that for Destination 2 we're supposed to increase our emergency saving to one month's living expenses and pay off the credit cards. We need help. What should we do first?"

"A lot of people ask that question, Matt," I replied. "Here's what you should do . . ."

KEEP ON TRUCKING . . . AND SAVING

If *you* have credit card debt, add half of the monthly surplus from your spending plan to your emergency savings and half to prepay your credit card debt. Once you've accumulated one month of living expenses in your emergency account, stop adding to the savings and apply the entire surplus to pay off your credit cards. If you pay off your credit cards first, add the entire monthly surplus to your emergency savings.

Determine the amount of one month's living expenses by using the average monthly living expense from your spending plan (page 126).

As you work toward Destination 2, continue contributing to your retirement account up to the amount your employer matches. For example, if your employer matches up to 3 percent of your income, contribute 3 percent of your income to retirement. But do it only if, and it is a *big IF*, you can still make steady progress on the Money Map. If you can't, temporarily stop your retirement contributions until you reach Destination 4.

> **HeyHoward@Crown.org**
>
> **QUESTION:** *Should I discontinue contributing to my retirement account until Destination 4?*
>
> **ANSWER:** *Contribute to your retirement account up to the amount your employer matches if you can still make steady progress on the Money Map.*

PAY OFF THE PLASTIC!

One of the biggest areas of conflict between Matt and Jennifer was their use of credit cards. They carried five cards between them and had maxed out three. They were using cash advances from some cards to satisfy the minimum monthly payments on others. The arrival of every credit card statement signaled the beginning of another verbal war between them.

This is common. The easy availability of credit has spawned a phenomenal growth in the number of cards held by consumers. In fact, surveys indicate the average cardholder has more than six credit cards, and the average household that has credit card

> **STARTLING STATS:**
>
> *The average American cardholder carries more than six credit cards, and the average household that has credit card debt owes more than $9,300 on their cards.*

debt owes more than $9,300 on their cards. The chart shows how credit card debt has grown.

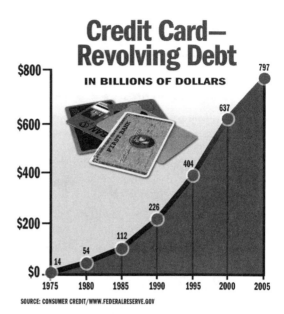

Credit Card—Revolving Debt

IN BILLIONS OF DOLLARS

SOURCE: CONSUMER CREDIT/WWW.FEDERALRESERVE.GOV

Part of the reason for the explosion in credit cards is the number of solicitations. There are now more than five *billion* credit card solicitations each year. Sometimes when I open my mailbox, it seemed as if we were receiving half of them!

Even worse, companies are now soliciting younger and younger people—from college students a few years ago to high school students today. And there is only one reason they want your business: *they make lots of money.*

Credit card companies also know that people spend about *one-third more* when they use credit cards rather than cash. Credit cards seem so painless, not like parting with *real* money. As one shopper said to another, "I like credit cards lots more than money because they go so much further—they're just plastic!"

About thirty-five million Americans pay only the required minimum each month, and many cardholders don't understand the financial consequences of paying only the minimum amount. No matter how good a deal they got on their purchase, how good does it feel twenty years later when they finally pay off their debt? If they pay only the monthly minimum at 18 percent interest, twenty years is about how long it takes. Some deal!

Here are some proven suggestions for paying off credit cards.

1. Perform plastic surgery.

When I analyze the financial situations of people in debt, I use a simple rule of thumb to determine whether credit cards are too dangerous for them. If they do not pay the entire balance at the end of each month, they need to perform some plastic surgery—any good scissors will do!

2. Limit the cards.

At one point, Bev and I had nine cards. Today we carry two that we pay in full and on time every month. We discovered that we don't need more than one or two cards. It is simpler for you to monitor the cards and to control your spending with just a couple of credit cards.

If you can't control your credit cards, perform some plastic surgery—any good scissors will do.

One key way to limit the temptations of additional cards and to make mealtime more peaceful is to opt out of receiving telemarketing calls and pre-approved credit card offers by mail. Log on the Web site of the National Do Not Call Registry at DoNotCall.gov to stop telemarketers. To stop junk mail, call toll free 1-(888)-5OPT-OUT. Everyone should do this!

3. Select the best credit cards for you.

About 6,000 financial institutions issue credit cards and compete for your business. If you have a good credit score, you will be able to choose among them. However, if you are reestablishing your credit history, you will have fewer options.

The key factors to help you choose the best credit card for you are the interest rate, the annual fees, and any incentives—such as frequent flyer miles—the card company may offer. Visit **CrownMoneyMap.org** for links to Web sites that will help you compare credit cards.

4. Snowball the credit cards.

"Which credit card should we pay off first?" Jennifer asked.

"Imagine that both of you have decided to build a large snowman," I answered.

"You start with a small snowball the size of your hand, which you roll in the snow. The first rotation of the snowball picks up just a little extra snow.

You can hardly tell it's grown in size. But you don't stop rolling it. You don't give up.

"You roll it over a second time and this time it collects more snow. Encouraged, you continue pushing together. Three turns . . . four . . . five . . . six . . . seven . . . You keep pushing. The snowball grows larger and larger with each turn.

"Now the size and momentum of the snowball begin working for you. Every time you roll the snowball over, it grows."

Matt and Jennifer were getting the picture. Over time, if you consistently reduce your debt load, your momentum of paying down principle keeps building. I call that the *Snowball Principle.*

THE SNOWBALL PRINCIPLE

The snowball illustrates several powerful principles of paying off debt.

- *If you are married, both spouses must push in the same direction.* To maximize your progress, husband and wife must agree and work together to become debt-free. This goes back to the goals you set together relating to your financial future. I suggest you write what you're agreeing to down on paper. That seals it in both your minds and ensures you'll be pushing hard in the same direction.

- *The initial effort is usually the most challenging.* Normally, it is not easy to become debt-free. You must be consistent month after month in your journey toward D-Day—Debtless Day. The more consistently you push against the debt snowball, the faster your momentum will increase.

- *The more you pay off debt, the more momentum you gain.* This is important to understand: You pay interest only on the *unpaid principal* balance. The faster you pay down your principal balance, the less you'll be paying in interest each month. As your principal decreases, fewer and fewer dollars from your monthly payment will be required to pay interest. More dollars each month will go toward paying down the principal.

Look at Jennifer and Matt's loan repayment schedule for their Visa card. They owe $5,300 at 14 percent interest with monthly payments of $100.

Month	Payment	Interest	Principal	Principal Balance
January	$100.00	$ 60.67	$ 39.33	$ 5,160.67
February	$100.00	$ 60.21	$ 39.79	$ 5,120.88
March	$100.00	$ 59.74	$ 40.25	$ 5,080.62
April	$100.00	$ 59.27	$ 40.73	$ 5,039.89
May	$100.00	$ 58.80	$ 41.20	$ 4,998.69
June	$100.00	$ 58.32	$ 41.68	$ 4,957.01

As their payment each month reduces the unpaid *principal balance*, less interest is charged the following month. Just like the snowball, with each rotation—a monthly payment of $100—the results are greater; more of the payment is applied to reducing principal. It starts out slowly and steadily picks up momentum until—the snowball becomes huge! By the time the Mitchells owe $500 on this debt, only $5.83 will go toward interest while $94.17 will go to reduce principal.

THE SNOWBALL STRATEGY

What is the most effective way to snowball yourself out of debt? How do you decide which debt to pay off first?

1. Pay off your smallest high-interest debt.

Review your credit card debts. In addition to making the minimum payments on *all* your credit cards, focus on accelerating the payment of your smallest high-interest credit card first. You will be encouraged as you make progress, finally eliminating that debt.

Then, after you pay off the first credit card, apply its payment toward the next smallest one. After the second credit card is paid off, apply what you were paying on the first and second toward the third smallest credit card debt, and so forth. That's the snowball principle in action!

Take whatever time is necessary to fill out "My Debt List" (next page). List your debts in order with the smallest remaining balance first. Every time you pay off a debt, draw a big line through it and celebrate!

2. Accelerate the snowball.

Once Bev and I started to snowball our debt, we got excited. We realized that if we could push a little harder, we would pay off our debts much faster. So we decided to sell things we didn't really need and apply the sales proceeds to our debt.

Many have cars, housing, or other expenses that cost too much. The payments are straining their spending plan and not allowing them to push the debt snowball forward. Make the hard decisions, live less expensively and crank up the speed on your snowball.

MY DEBT LIST
SNOWBALLING MY WAY TO DEBT-FREE LIVING!

Date:_____

Credit Card Debt

Lender	Balance Remaining	Minimum Payment	New Payment	Payments Remaining	Interest Rate
_____	_____	_____	_____	_____	_____
_____	_____	_____	_____	_____	_____
_____	_____	_____	_____	_____	_____
_____	_____	_____	_____	_____	_____
_____	_____	_____	_____	_____	_____
_____	_____	_____	_____	_____	_____
_____	_____	_____	_____	_____	_____
_____	_____	_____	_____	_____	_____
_____	_____	_____	_____	_____	_____
_____	_____	_____	_____	_____	_____
_____	_____	_____	_____	_____	_____

Consumer Debt (all debts other than credit cards, home mortgages, and business loans)

_____	_____	_____	_____	_____	_____
_____	_____	_____	_____	_____	_____
_____	_____	_____	_____	_____	_____
_____	_____	_____	_____	_____	_____
_____	_____	_____	_____	_____	_____
_____	_____	_____	_____	_____	_____
_____	_____	_____	_____	_____	_____
_____	_____	_____	_____	_____	_____
_____	_____	_____	_____	_____	_____

Home Mortgages

_____	_____	_____	_____	_____	_____
_____	_____	_____	_____	_____	_____
_____	_____	_____	_____	_____	_____

Business Debt

_____	_____	_____	_____	_____	_____
_____	_____	_____	_____	_____	_____
_____	_____	_____	_____	_____	_____

136

3. Transfer balances to another credit card.

If you carry credit card balances at high interest rates, consider transferring the balance to a card that charges *less* interest. That can save a lot of money. But before transferring to a lower-rate card, confirm that the new card has no transfer fee, no annual fee, and that the interest rate on transferred balances is not higher than the advertised rate; sometimes the low rate offer is only for purchases. And remember, if you miss a payment or make a payment late, your interest rate will automatically skyrocket in most cases.

4. Develop a debt repayment schedule.

I recommend that you prepare a debt repayment schedule for every debt that you focus on paying off early. It will help you stay on top of your progress.

ABOUT YOUR CREDIT SCORE

Your credit score (FICO score) determines whether you can get credit. And your score may be high enough to get credit but not high enough to get a decent interest rate—whether you're looking for a mortgage, a credit card, a car loan, or some other type of credit. Without good scores, your application to rent an apartment may be turned down. Your scores can affect your car insurance premiums and in some cases even getting a job.

A credit score is a number designed to help lenders and others measure your likelihood of making payments on time. The FICO score ranges from 300–850, with the average score around 680. Higher scores are better. FICO scores above 700 indicate a good credit risk, while scores below 600 indicate a poor risk.

A low score can lead to much higher interest rates. For example, if you apply for a thirty-year home mortgage and your credit score is too low, you could pay as much as 3 percent more. On a $100,000 mortgage, that 3 percent difference will cost you $200 per month. Over the life of the loan it adds up to $72,000!

The primary things that will harm your credit score are late payments or non-payments of bills or debts, bankruptcy, foreclosure, repossession, bills or loans sent to collection. Your credit score will also be affected if your credit history is short, or if you have maxed out your credit limits. To improve your credit score, the two most important actions you can take are to pay your bills on time and reduce your total debt. Once you start doing this, your score will begin to improve in about three months. Look at the factors affecting your score.

How FICO Credit Scores Are Determined
Factors that go into a credit score, and how they're weighted

Payment history
For credit cards, retail accounts, car loans, mortgages, and similar debts.

Amount owed
The number of accounts with balances, and the amount you owe vs. the amount of credit available. Maxing out credit cards lowers your score.

35% **30%** **15%** **10%** **10%**

Credit history
How long you've had each account. The longer your credit history, the better.

Types of credit used
Number of credit cards, retail accounts, mortgages, and other accounts.

New credit
Number of recently opened accounts and recent inquiries. Opening several accounts in a short period can hurt your score.

SOURCE: USA Today Research

YOUR CREDIT REPORT

Your credit score is based on the information contained in your credit report. Late or missed payments, foreclosures or repossessions remain part of your credit report for seven years. You'll have to wait ten years for a bankruptcy to be removed, and fifteen years for a tax lien. Even though these remain on your credit report, over time they have less impact if you pay your bills on time and reduce your debt.

Everyone should get a copy of their credit report once every twelve months. To order a free copy, log on to AnnualCreditReport.com

Everyone should get a copy of their credit report once a year. Review it to make sure there are no mistakes or that you have not been the victim of identity theft. You can order a free copy of your credit report once every twelve months. To order, log on to AnnualCreditReport.com or call toll free 877–322–8228.

The free copy of your credit report does not contain your credit score. Unless you are applying for a home mortgage or home equity loan, you will pay to receive your score. Any of the three main credit agencies will sell you your score.

Roadside Assistance—Online!

For *automated debt repayment schedules,* go to **CrownMoneyMap.org**.

Visit the Web site for links to compare credit card rates and for more information on how to improve your *credit score.*

3 MAKING PROGRESS ON THE JOURNEY

My husband is active in the military and was deployed in Iraq. I stayed home with our six children, cashing in the military paychecks as they arrived—which included extra combat pay. I found myself in the new position of having to manage my family's finances instead of my husband.

When my husband left for Iraq, we had $58,000 in mostly credit card debt. Without telling my husband, I followed the Money Map and used the extra income to set aside $1,000 for emergencies and pay down our debt. I believed this was the right thing to do, but I wanted to make sure.

I called in to Crown's *Money Matters* radio program and told Howard Dayton about my dilemma and asked, "What should I do with the excess? Give it as an offering to God, continue paying down my debt, or save for our family vacation?"

Howard suggested that we do all three—give generously to God, continue paying down the debt, and celebrate with a family vacation. He also said that we should also use this challenging time to bring our marriage closer together once he returned.

When my husband returned home for Christmas furlough, I told him everything that I had done. I showed him a jar full of our shredded plastic credit cards and a fist full of paid off credit card statements—and he was thrilled with my decision! Along with his income and my work, we are continuing to cruise through Destination 2 on our way to true financial freedom! In a few months, we should have our entire debt paid off and pay cash for our family vacation. God is good!

—**ROBBIE LANGHALS,** *Colorado Springs, Colorado*

Read and watch more stories along the journey at CrownMoneyMap.org.

DISCUSSION QUESTIONS

1. Have you been successful in saving regularly? Why? If needed, what will you do to improve?

2. Are you a wise, careful spender? If not, why not?

3. Describe your *mind-set* concerning giving, spending, saving, and debt. Does anything need to change? If so, what will you do?

4. When someone mentions the word *budget*, what do you think of? If you are not using a spending plan, what will you do about it?

5. If you have credit card debt, describe how it would feel to have it paid off completely. Explain how you will implement the snowball principle with your credit card debt.

6. What did you learn from this section that was most helpful to you? Why was it helpful?

 **TOOLS FOR YOUR JOURNEY**

Helping you start a spending plan (budget)

- *Crown Money Map™ Financial Software.* This PC-based budgeting software does more than track income, expenses, and investments; it will teach you biblical principles for managing money during the budgeting process.

- *Crown Mvelopes™ Personal.* This secure, Web-based budgeting software is conveniently available online anytime, anywhere with the ability to track your spending automatically with each transaction.

- *Family Financial Workbook.* This budgeting workbook is ideal for those who prefer using pencil and paper.

- *Cash Organizer.* This handy binder contains envelopes that represent each budgeting category. It is perfect for those that are learning the discipline of budgeting or for those who do their spending in cash.

Helping you get out of debt

To get more detailed help on becoming debt free, read my book *Free and Clear* (Chicago: Moody, 2006).

PART

4

DESTINATIONS 3 and 4

We have so much debt in our nation that the average person has been described as someone driving on a bond-financed highway, in a bank-financed car, fueled by credit-card-financed gasoline, going to purchase furniture on the installment plan to put in his mortgaged-to-the-hilt home.

— ANONYMOUS

CHAPTER 14

DESTINATION 3:
CONSUMER DEBT PAID OFF

Early one evening there was a knock at the door. To my surprise, it was Matt and Jennifer Mitchell, carrying a basket and smiling ear to ear. Although we had talked on the phone a couple of times, we had not seen them for months.

"Surprise!" Matt exclaimed. "I hope this is convenient, because we've come to celebrate! Jennifer checked your schedule with Bev, but we asked her to keep it a secret."

"Sure, great to see you! But I'm stumped. What's the occasion?"

"Well, we haven't seen you in a while," Jennifer said as she reached to hug Bev. "And like Matt said, we're here to celebrate. And ask a few questions, of course."

"Well, let's head to the kitchen and see what's in the basket," Bev said, with her excitement matching my curiosity.

"Remember the last time we met to celebrate?" Matt asked. "In the ice-cream shop?"

"I sure do," I said. "You had one of the biggest sundaes on the planet!

And even better than that, you'd reached Destination 1."

"So welcome us to Destination 2," Matt said. "This time we'll make the sundaes."

"You've finished paying off all of the credit cards?" I asked in disbelief.

"And increased our savings to equal one month of living expenses!" Jennifer said. "And that's not all!"

"We've got everything we need here for the world's greatest sundaes," Matt said, pulling out ice cream and bananas and nuts and jars of toppings. Last of all, he pulled out a jar of pickles. "And Jennifer asked for these!"

"You're expecting!" Bev exclaimed. She hugged Jennifer as though she were her own daughter. "That's wonderful! Howard, can you believe it?"

"Congratulations, Matt!" I said, reaching to shake his hand. "Wow! Let's celebrate reaching Destination 2 and having your third child.

"Okay, Matt," I said as we later sat down around the table. "Tell us how you were able to get to Destination 2 a year earlier than scheduled." The Mitchells had hoped to pay off their credit cards in three years, but it had taken only two.

"Well," Matt started. "We were faithful to do our part, and God was more than faithful to do His part. We were able to trim our expenses even further than we first thought."

"And then," Jennifer excitedly interrupted, "the Lord enabled Matt to earn even more at his job than we expected, and we put it toward paying off the credit cards."

Now they were ready to start on their trip to Destination 3—saving three months' living expenses in an emergency fund and paying off their consumer debt. They had questions. How should they divide their monthly surplus between saving and debt repayment? Exactly what is a consumer debt? Which consumer debt should they try to pay off first?

KEEP ON . . . KEEPING ON

When you arrive at Destination 2, you have accumulated an emergency fund equal to one month of living expenses. Now you are going to increase your emergency savings to three months of your living expenses.

Use exactly the same strategy recommended for Destination 2. Add half of your monthly surplus from your spending plan to your emergency savings and half to prepay your consumer debt. When you've reached the goal of three months' worth of expenses in your emergency fund, stop adding to it. Instead, apply the entire surplus to pay off your consumer debts. If you pay off your consumer debts first, add the entire surplus to your emergency savings until you reach that goal.

SNOWBALL THE CONSUMER DEBT

Consumer debt is all debt other than credit card debt, the home mortgage, and business loans.

How do you decide which consumer debt to pay off first? The same way you decided which credit card to pay off first. Continue making the minimum payments on all your consumer debts, but focus on accelerating the payment of your smallest higher-interest consumer debt first.

Then, after you pay off the first consumer debt, apply its payment toward the next smallest one. After the second one is paid off, apply what

you were paying on the first and second toward the third smallest consumer debt, and so forth. Snowball your consumer debt.

The three most common consumer debts are auto debt, student loans, and home equity loans, including home equity lines of credit.

PAYING OFF AUTO DEBT

Car debt is one of the biggest obstacles for most people on their journey to true financial freedom because most people never get out of it. Just when they are ready to pay off a car, they trade it in and purchase a newer one with credit.

Unlike a home, which usually appreciates in value, the moment you drive a car off the lot it *depreciates* in value. It's worth less than you paid for it.

Take these four steps to get out of auto debt:

HeyHoward@Crown.org

QUESTION: *Why is it so important to pay off my car debt?*
ANSWER: *Most people have car debt all their lives with monthly payments averaging about $375. Invest that amount from age twenty-one to sixty-five, and it would grow to about $4 million!*

1. Decide to keep your car at least three years longer than your car loan.
2. Pay off your car loan.
3. After your last payment, keep making the payment, but pay it to yourself. Put it into an account that you will use to buy your next car.
4. When you are ready to replace your car, the cash you have saved plus your car's trade-in value should be sufficient to buy a car without credit. It may not be a new car, but a newer low-mileage used car without any debt is a better value anyway.

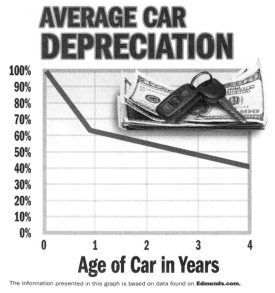

AVERAGE CAR DEPRECIATION

Age of Car in Years

The information presented in this graph is based on data found on **Edmunds.com.**

Lean against the Culture

Bev and I realized that if we were going to experience true financial freedom, we would need to get out of car debt—for good!

So we chose to buy used cars rather than new ones, avoiding the worst depreciation loss any car experiences—the first two years. That rapid depreciation is why so many new car buyers are upside down on their auto loans—owing more than the car is worth. Look at the graph to see how quickly cars lose value.

Bev and I decided to keep our cars as long as they were safe to drive. As Crown's cofounder, Larry Burkett, used to say, "The most economical car is usually the one you already own." Because these decisions were so countercultural, it was important to have a good sense of humor concerning our cars. We laughed at the cars and ourselves . . . all the way to the bank.

I once bought a truck that cost only $100—and it looked it! A neighbor felt sorry for me and borrowed the truck and had it painted. Suddenly it looked like a $200 truck! It was not much of a status symbol, but I really enjoyed driving it and never worried about someone putting another dent in it. Pay off your car and stay out of auto debt. It is a major step toward enjoying true financial freedom.

> ## STARTLING STATS:
>
> *"A new $28,000 car will lose about $17,000 of value in the first four years you own it. To get the same result, you could toss a $100 bill out the car window once a week."*
> — DAVE RAMSEY

AUTOMOBILE LEASING—JUST ANOTHER NAME FOR DEBT

Leasing has become a popular alternative to buying a car. The attraction is that lease payments are usually lower than purchase payments, making it look as though you're getting more for less. You're NOT!

There are some huge downsides to leasing. At the end of a purchase loan, you own the car, but at the end of a lease, you own *nothing*. When you return the car, you may be socked with charges for excessive mileage to the tune of ten to twenty cents a mile and penalties for wear and tear.

It also can be very expensive, if not impossible, to get out of a car lease early. An auto lease agreement is just another name for debt; avoid it!

> *The cost of gas is only 25 percent of the cost of driving your car. So, every time you fill up, multiply the cost of gas by four to figure out what you're really spending.*

THE COST OF DRIVING

With the cost of gasoline these days, I don't have to tell you that it's *expensive* to operate your auto. But this may surprise you: Gas isn't the biggest expense. If you get twenty miles to the gallon and a gallon of gas costs $3.00, your fuel cost is fifteen cents a mile. However, according to a Hertz Rental Car survey, when you add insurance, tires, depreciation, license, and repairs, it all adds up to more than sixty cents a mile! The cost of gas is only 25 percent of the cost of driving your car.

So, every time you fill up, multiply the cost of gas by four to figure out what you're really spending. If you want to cut your car expenses, carpool or do all your shopping in one trip. Remember, every mile you don't drive, you save yourself more than 60 cents. One hundred miles means sixty dollars!

PAYING OFF STUDENT LOANS

Student loans are rising dramatically. Just look at the graph "Average Stu-

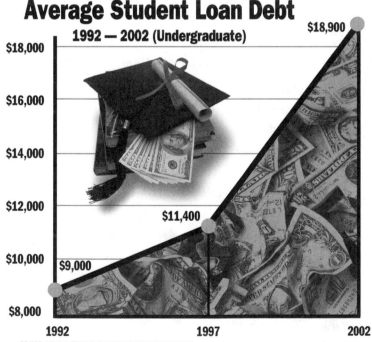

Average Student Loan Debt

1992 — 2002 (Undergraduate)

$18,900

$18,000

$16,000

$14,000

$12,000

$11,400

$10,000

$9,000

$8,000

1992   1997   2002

SOURCE: NATIONAL STUDENT LOAN SURVEYS, WWW.NELLIEMAE.COM

dent Loan Debt."

Student loans come from two sources: the government and private lenders. The government usually offers the lower interest rates because they want to encourage college attendance. They subsidize the loans to drive down the cost.

The day always comes when student loans must be repaid. If you are feeling pressured by them, where can you go for help? If you have more than one school loan, consolidating them may be a good option. It may reduce your interest rate and lower your monthly payment.

"I can't retire! I haven't paid off my student loan yet."

From the Wall Street Journal—permission, Cartoon Features Syndicate.

The government has established an excellent Web site that will allow you to apply for student loan consolidation directly over the Internet. The Web site is LoanConsolidation.ed.gov.

Each year on July 1, the Department of Education adjusts the interest rates charged for school loans. If you are considering consolidation when interest rates are rising, apply for consolidation before July 1. If interest rates are falling, wait until after this date.

HOME EQUITY LOANS

Home equity loans are simply additional mortgages. They use the equity in your home as the collateral that secures the loan. There are two main ways to tap into your home equity: through a home equity loan (second mortgage) or a home equity line of credit.

Home equity loans are attractive because lenders often charge a lower interest rate and spread the repayment over a longer period of time. This means that the monthly payment becomes smaller yet. Tax-deductible interest is another carrot lenders use to entice homeowners into using their home equity to fund major purchases or consolidate debt. If you itemize your taxes, you can deduct the interest paid on home equity loans. There are limitations, however. Consult your tax advisor for guidance.

Don't secure a home equity loan without understanding the risks and costs. If you cannot pay a credit card bill, the issuer can take you to court and sue you for recovery. With a home equity loan, however, failure to pay could cost you your home.

Fees and closing costs on a home equity loan can range from nothing to thousands of dollars. When there are no closing costs, however, there is usually some sort of catch such as a higher rate or a prepayment penalty.

HOME EQUITY LINE OF CREDIT

With a home equity line of credit (HELOC), the lender approves you for a loan up to a certain amount, allowing you to borrow up to this "credit limit." Think of a HELOC as a *giant credit card*. You can borrow whenever you want and as much as you want—up to the credit limit. Your monthly payments are based on the amount you actually borrow.

Several of the advantages of a HELOC are similar to a home equity loan: lower interest rates, tax-deductible interest, and lower closing costs than with refinancing a mortgage. The major downside to using a HELOC is that it can be a *huge* temptation. Just like a credit card, the tendency is to use it too often rather than spending carefully.

CONSOLIDATING YOUR LOANS

In theory, consolidating a number of higher-interest loans into one lower-interest loan makes a lot of sense. Consolidated loans typically offer lower monthly payments, and making just one payment is simpler.

If you have outstanding credit card balances, student loans, auto payments, and mortgages, you may be a candidate for loan consolidation. You have many options from which to choose: taking a personal loan from your bank or credit union, rolling your credit-card balances to a low-rate card, or borrowing against the equity in your home.

There is one huge downside in consolidating your loans, however. Are you ready? Here it is. If you haven't solved the problems that put you into debt in the first place, you'll end up worse off—and probably much worse off. Surveys confirm that about two-thirds of those who borrow against their home equity to pay off credit cards run up more credit card debt within two years.

If you cannot regularly spend less than you earn, you will continue racking up new debt. You will have to wrestle with not only the consolidation loan but also with these new debts. So, as attractive as the idea is, people should not consolidate until they have changed their habits and have a monthly surplus.

© Kings Features Syndicate. Used by permission.

Do yourself a favor: Hate debt; start paying it off; spend less than you earn. Then consolidate your loans.

DEALING WITH CREDITORS

Many people who get deep in debt develop an attitude that says, "If I ignore the problem, it will eventually go away." But the problem will not go away, in fact, it will intensify. Most creditors are very open to hearing from you and often are willing to work out some arrangement for you to repay. However, it is almost impossible to negotiate with a creditor you have ignored. Silence is deadly. The key is good communication.

It is best to run toward your creditors, not away from them. As hard and embarrassing as it may be, always take the initiative in keeping your lenders informed.

There are three simple rules to follow when dealing with creditors:

1. Start communicating with your creditors.
2. Offer lenders a written copy of your budget, a list of your debts, and your repayment plan.
3. Exercise integrity—always be completely honest with your creditors.

For more tips on these strategies, see my book *Free and Clear*, pages 96–98.

DEBT MANAGEMENT COMPANIES

One option for helping you work out a repayment plan is to use a debt management company who will represent you to negotiate lower monthly payments and lower interest rates with major credit card companies and certain other creditors. Additional benefits are that you make one monthly payment rather than many, and you stop additional late fees and new over-the-credit-limit fees.

Unfortunately, there are many scam artists in the business of debt negotiations. You must be very careful to deal only with reputable companies. Interview the companies you are considering and compare charges. One of the very best is FinancialHope.com.

BANKRUPTCY

Twenty years ago one out of every three-hundred households went bankrupt. This year about one out of every sixty-nine will go under. If this year's number holds steady, *one of every seven households in the United States would declare bankruptcy* during the next ten years.

The Bible never prohibits bankruptcy, but it does discourage it: *"The wicked borrow and do not repay, but the righteous give generously."* [1] Make every effort to avoid bankruptcy. However, I believe bankruptcy to be permissible if the borrower experiences such extreme financial difficulties that there is no option, or if the emotional health of the borrower is at stake.

Bankruptcy is not the easy, quick fix that some think. It destroys your credit and remains on your credit report for *ten* years. But that's not the end of it; many job applications ask if you have *ever* filed for bankruptcy.

Although we discourage bankruptcy, it can provide the opportunity for people to regain their financial stability. If you've declared bankruptcy, don't carry a load of guilt. Learn what the Lord wants to teach you from the difficult experience. And—I hope you're ready for this—even though you may no longer be *legally* obligated to repay the debts, you should try to repay them. That's what God really desires.

Repaying your debts will develop your character and you will be a godly example to your creditors. Interestingly, some of the most successful people I know in business—and in life—have made the decision to repay debts extinguished by bankruptcy.

COSIGNING

Cosigning is risky business. A Federal Trade Commission study found that 50 percent of those who cosigned for bank loans ended up making the payments. And 75 percent of those who cosigned for finance company loans ended up making the payments! So, if you cosign, you are likely to pay, and that's not all. Your credit will be damaged because lenders normally do not contact you when payments are late or they repossess a car. By the time they ask you to pay the debt, it is too late to protect your credit.

The Bible says, "It is poor judgment to co-sign a friend's note, to become responsible for a neighbor's debts." The phrase "poor judgment" is literally translated "destitute of mind." Do not cosign!

Cosigning relates to debt. *Anytime you cosign, you become legally responsible for the debt of another.* You are not just acting as a reference; you are promising to pay back the entire loan if the borrower defaults. It's just as if you borrowed the money and *gave* it to your friend or relative who is asking you to cosign. You are completely responsible for the debt.

The Bible is clear: *"It is poor judgment to co-sign a friend's note, to become responsible for a neighbor's debts."*[2] The phrase "poor judgment" is literally translated "destitute of mind!" So please, *never* cosign a loan.

Parents should not cosign for their children, either. You remain responsible for their debt, and by not cosigning, you model for your children that cosigning should be avoided. Parents often cosign for their children's first car. Bev and I decided not to do this. Instead, we encouraged them to save for the purchase of their first car by matching a portion of what they saved. For more on cosigning, see *Free and Clear*, chapter 17 (especially pages 168–170).

Depending upon the amount of consumer debt you have, it may take a while to wipe it out completely. Don't be discouraged. It's worth the effort. Remain focused on getting rid of it and on to the next stop on your journey to *true financial freedom*—Destination 4.

Roadside Assistance—Online!

Have questions about your consumer debt? Visit the FAQ section of Crown MoneyMap.org.

I know the advantages of the eighth wonder of the world—compounding.

—BARON ROTHSCHILD

Financier

CHAPTER 15

DESTINATION 4:

SAVING FOR MAJOR PURCHASES

We received a postcard from Matt and Jennifer. They were spending a day at the beach with their children, celebrating their arrival at Destination 3—ahead of schedule!

We met with them a week later, and they were still excited. "We've made big-time progress," Matt shared.

"And we've not only improved financially, but we're communicating better," Jennifer added, looking at Matt. "It's been a while since we've argued about money; that's definitely helped our marriage."

"That's such good news," Bev said. "Are you ready to tackle Destination 4?"

"We sure are!" Matt responded with conviction. "We know that at Destination 4 we focus on saving for our big-ticket items like retirement, the kids' education, and our business. But how do we decide which to do first?"

"Good question, Matt," I answered. "As you know, the first three destinations on your Money Map focus on establishing your spending plan, building up your emergency savings, and getting out of credit card and consumer debt.

"By now you've started to build a solid financial foundation. You're ready to turn the corner from aggressive debt repayment to aggressive saving. The money you were paying on the credit card and consumer debt is now available to save for your most important future needs. Let's review the possibilities."

MAJOR FUTURE PURCHASES

The Crown Money Map divides saving for future needs into four categories.

1. Major purchases such as a home or car
2. Children's education
3. Retirement
4. Starting a business

Saving Priorities

To establish the order in which you will save for future needs, review your life purpose and goals. They will help guide how you choose to allocate your savings.

Since Matt and Jennifer already owned their home, they didn't need to save for a down payment. They did, however, choose to continue making the car payment on their paid-off car, writing the check to their own savings account for their next car purchase.

Their top priority was funding the start of Matt's business. They decided to allocate their savings this way: 20 percent for retirement, 20 percent for their children's education, and 60 percent to start the car business.

Reasonable Down Payment on Home

Many people put little or no money down when they purchase their homes. Instead, I encourage you to save enough for a *reasonable* down payment, at least 20 percent of the purchase price.

There are several advantages to this approach. First, your mortgage and monthly payments will be smaller. Second, it eliminates the need for you to carry expensive mortgage insurance (PMI) that protects only the lender. Third, your smaller payments make it easier to afford larger prepayments, speeding up the day when you can burn your mortgage. Fourth, starting with at least 20 percent equity protects you. Many people who have bought a home without a reasonable down payment have sold it, only to discover that they owed more than they could get for it—especially after paying selling expenses.

PRINCIPLES FOR SAVING

As you begin saving for future purchases, keep in mind these principles for saving.

1. Steady saving adds up.

When you are in debt, interest is *not* your friend. You must work to earn an income to pay for the cost of interest. However, when you get out of debt and begin to save, interest becomes your ally. It works *for* you. For example, if you start with $2,000 and save $500 a month earning 7 percent, in ten years it will grow to $90,561. By the end of the tenth year, it will be earning $528 a month in interest. It is working for you.

2. Compounding is a friend.

Wealthy Baron Rothschild was once asked if he had seen the seven wonders of the world. He responded, "No, but I know the advantages of the eighth wonder of the world—compounding." Compounding occurs when the interest you earn is added to the principle, and *both* earn interest. This produces a powerful snowball effect. There are three variables in compounding: the *amount* you save, the *rate* you earn on your savings, and the length of *time* you save.

> *"Compounding is the greatest mathematical discovery of all time, not E=mc²."*
>
> ALBERT EINSTEIN

    1. *The amount.* The amount you save will be determined by your income, how well you control your spending, and how much debt you have.

The amount you have available for saving should increase as you progress on your Money Map.

2. *The rate of return.* The second variable is the rate of return you earn on your savings and investments. The following table demonstrates how an investment of $1,000 per year grows at various rates. As you can see, an increase in the rate of return has a remarkable effect on the amount accumulated. A 2 percent increase almost doubles the amount over forty years.

RATES OF RETURN OVER THE SHORT AND LONG TERM

Percent Earned	Year 5	Year 10	Year 20	Year 30	Year 40
6%	5,813	13,656	38,502	83,706	165,950
8%	6,123	15,245	49,083	124,192	290,906
10%	6,453	17,070	63,278	188,366	526,985
12%	6,816	19,169	82,435	291,235	980,358

HeyHoward@Crown.org

QUESTION: *I'm fifty-five years old. Is it too late for me to begin to save and invest?*
ANSWER: *Absolutely not! No way! It's never too late to begin to apply God's financial principles. The key is simply to be faithful starting today.*

3. *The time.* Answer this question: Who do you think accumulated more by age sixty-five—Alice, who started saving $1,000 a year at age twenty-one for eight years and then completely stopped—or Ben, who saved $1,000 a year for thirty-seven years but started at age twenty-nine? Both earned 10 percent. Is it Alice, who contributed a total of $8,000 or Ben, who contributed $37,000? Look at the chart "The Impact of Compounding" on page 163.

Incredibly, it's Alice, who contributed a total of only $8,000—$29,000 less than Ben! Thanks to compounding Alice accumulated $64,693 more because she started saving earlier. The *sooner* you start saving, the better!

THE IMPACT OF COMPOUNDING

	Alice			*Ben*	
Age	Contribution	Year-end Value		Contribution	Year-end Value
21	1,000	1,100		0	0
22	1,000	2,310		0	0
23	1,000	3,641		0	0
24	1,000	5,105		0	0
25	1,000	6,716		0	0
26	1,000	8,487		0	0
27	1,000	10,436		0	0
28	1,000	12,579		0	0
29	0	13,837		1,000	1,100
30	0	15,221		1,000	2,310
31	0	16,743		1,000	3,641
32	0	18,417		1,000	5,105
33	0	20,259		1,000	6,716
34	0	22,284		1,000	8,487
35	0	24,513		1,000	10,436
36	0	26,964		1,000	12,579
37	0	29,661		1,000	14,937
38	0	32,627		1,000	17,531
39	0	35,889		1,000	20,384
40	0	39,478		1,000	23,523
41	0	43,426		1,000	26,975
42	0	47,769		1,000	30,772
43	0	52,546		1,000	34,950
44	0	57,800		1,000	39,545
45	0	63,580		1,000	44,599
46	0	69,938		1,000	50,159
47	0	76,932		1,000	56,275
48	0	84,625		1,000	63,003
49	0	93,088		1,000	70,403
50	0	103,397		1,000	78,543
51	0	112,636		1,000	87,497
52	0	123,898		1,000	97,347
53	0	136,290		1,000	108,182
54	0	149,919		1,000	120,100
55	0	164,911		1,000	133,210
56	0	181,402		1,000	147,631
57	0	199,542		1,000	163,494
58	0	219,496		1,000	180,943
59	0	241,446		1,000	200,138
60	0	265,590		1,000	221,252
61	0	292,149		1,000	244,477
62	0	321,364		1,000	270,024
63	0	353,501		1,000	298,127
64	0	388,851		1,000	329,039
65	0	427,736		1,000	363,043
	8,000			37,000	

The graph below may help you better visualize the benefits of starting now. If a person saves $2.74 a day—$1,000 a year—and earns 10 percent, at the end of forty years the savings will grow to $526,985 and will be earning $4,392 each month. However, if the same person waits one year before starting, then saves for 39 years, the result will be $50,899 *less*. Start saving today!

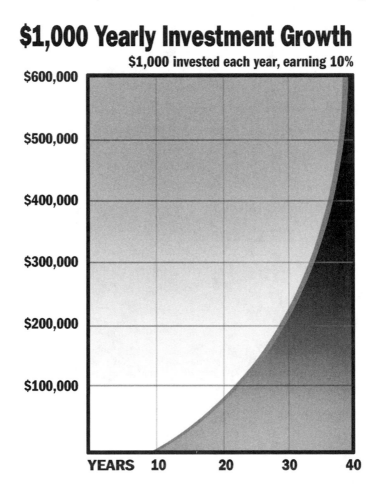

$1,000 Yearly Investment Growth
$1,000 invested each year, earning 10%

CHILDREN'S EDUCATION

Debt among college students is skyrocketing. The average graduating senior has about $19,000[1] in school loans and $3,300 in credit card debt plus what they owe for their wheels. Those who finish graduate school owe an average of $39,000. This debt forces some into jobs they would not otherwise choose. They realize too late that *"the borrower is servant to the lender."*[2]

Avoiding School Debt

Paying for a college education is a great opportunity for parents and children to grow closer to each other and to the Lord. As soon as children are old enough, pray together each week for God to provide funds for their education. Ask God for solutions that will eliminate or reduce the need to borrow. And then watch! He is eager to reveal Himself to each of us by answering our prayers.

It is a blessing when parents are able to save to help pay for their children's education. There are several educational savings options: state-sponsored 529 Plans and Prepaid Tuition Plans, Coverdell Educational Savings Accounts, and Roth IRAs. Each of these options has pros and cons. Log on to the Money Map Web site for a current explanation of each, along with links to Web sites containing helpful information on student grants and scholarships.

Many parents and grandparents are not in a financial position to fund any part of their children's education. If you're one of them—*don't feel guilty!* You can only do what you can do, and this may be a blessing in disguise.

What Children Can Do

When children are old enough, have them work to save for their college. When they enter college, encourage them to work part-time, and don't forget summer jobs. When students work to pay for college, they appreciate it more, are more serious about their studies, and develop a solid work ethic.

Larry Burkett, cofounder of Crown Financial Ministries, worked his way through college. Although it took him six years instead of four because of his work schedule, it cemented the habits of hard work and careful budgeting. These habits were his most valuable lessons of college.

Another option is to attend a community college near home for the first two years. This is less expensive than enrolling in a four-year college, especially if it is possible for the student to live at home.

This should be your objective: encourage children to graduate from college with *little* or *no* school debt.

INVESTING FOR RETIREMENT

Retirement has become a time of *broken promises.* Every year more than a hundred companies break their promises to provide a pension to their employees. Social Security is projected to run out of money. The bottom line: Don't rely solely on an employer or the government; *you* need to invest for your retirement.

When investing for retirement I recommend a simple rule of thumb: *First, take advantage of all employer matches, and second, invest in a Roth IRA or Roth 401k.*

If your employer offers to match your contribution, do it! It's free money. For example, if your employer will match up to 3 percent of your salary in a 401k contribution, make sure you put at least 3 percent in. It's that simple.

If you do not have a match, or once you have contributed for the match, focus on funding a Roth IRA. I am a huge fan of the Roth. Although your contributions to a Roth are not tax deductible, they grow *tax free*, and after age 59½, all withdrawals are *tax free!* Many choose the traditional IRA, because contributions are tax deductible, however, the downside is that one pays income tax on all withdrawals. I don't know what the tax rate will be in the future, but the government's deficit spending could force it much higher than it is today. This will be a huge advantage to using a Roth.

> ### STARTLING STATS:
>
> A whopping 97 percent of Americans age sixty-five have less than $600 in their checking account. Only 3 percent are financially secure, and 54 percent are still working, according to USA Today.

Each year you (and your spouse if you are married) can invest $4,000 to $5,000 in a Roth IRA. Since there are limitations based on age and income level, check with your tax preparer to determine your personal maximum.

Roadside Assistance—Online!

For more help on *retirement investing*, visit **CrownMoneyMap.org**.

Build your business before building your house.
— KING SOLOMON

DESTINATION 4:

SAVING TO START YOUR OWN BUSINESS

Matt took the day off from work, and he and Jennifer invited us out for lunch.

Jennifer began. "We're so excited about the progress we've made. We can't believe we have three months of living expenses saved."

"And the credit card debts, car loans, and student loans are history. They're gone!" Matt interrupted, grinning broadly. "The Lord has done so much for us."

"Well, as you know, it's been my dream to own an auto dealership someday," Matt continued. "And Destination 4 on the Money Map is where we begin saving to start a business. I know we've talked about this before, but it still just doesn't seem realistic," Matt said, shaking his head in disbelief. "How can we ever save enough to buy one?"

I nodded. "I understand how you feel, but never underestimate what God can do. The Bible says that He *'is able to do far more than we would ever dare to ask or even dream of.'*[1]

"Remember, your responsibility is to be faithful to handle money God's way and save as much as you can. Once you've done that, you can be content and wait for the Lord to do what He wants in His own time, which is always the best. And while you're saving the money, you'll need to continue to do a lot of homework to prepare if you expect to make a go of it."

A COUNTRY OF ENTREPRENEURS

A recent survey found that 72 percent of Americans have considered starting a business, and 51 percent of those would like to launch one within the next five years.[2]

If you sense that God may be leading you to start your own business someday, there are several steps you should take to position yourself to succeed.

1. Prepare yourself financially.

The reason for waiting until Destination 4 to begin saving for a business is that it is important to have your *personal* finances as stable as possible. When you no longer have credit card or consumer debts, your monthly expenses are lower. And having set aside three month's living expenses (at Destination 3), you have a margin in case you need income from the business during some of its lean months.

This may surprise you: It is preferable to start your business *before* you buy your home. The Bible says, *"Develop your business first before building your house."*[3] In other words, create your source of income; then acquire your home.

One of the most common reasons for the failure of start-up businesses is lack of capital—not enough cash saved up. When you begin a business with lots of borrowed money, you invite added pressure to be profitable quickly. Many businesses require several years to become profitable.

These are my recommendations:

- Be patient!
- Save as much as you need before launching your business.
- Use as little business debt as possible, and pay it off as quickly as possible.

When you operate with little or no debt, you have a competitive edge against businesses saddled with large monthly payments. You also have more financial stability to weather unexpected challenges.

> **STARTLING STATS:**
>
> *About 80 percent of all business start-ups—four of every five—do not survive beyond the second year.*

2. Identify a good business opportunity.

Research business opportunities for which you are well suited—ones that you think you would enjoy, that you can afford to start, and that meet your personal goals. When you discover one, gain some experience in the business before launching into ownership.

3. Pray for a mentor.

Ask God to provide you a mentor who really understands the business you are considering. I did this when I started in real estate, and it was the *best* decision of my business career. I took a cut in pay to work for my mentor, but it was well worth it. He was so experienced that he taught me more in two years than I could have learned in ten years doing it on my own.

"Matt, that's exactly what's happened to you!" Jennifer said with a look of surprise. "Mr. Johnson has become your mentor."

"I hadn't thought of it before," said Matt, rubbing his chin and reflecting on his employer. "But you're right. He's investing a lot of time teaching me the business, and we've become real close friends."

> **HeyHoward@Crown.org**
>
> **QUESTION:** *I like to cook and want to open a restaurant. What advice can you give me?*
> **ANSWER:** *There is a world of difference between liking to cook and owning a restaurant. When starting any business, it is important to either have lots of experience yourself or a mentor who has it.*

4. Draft a business plan.

Unfortunately, 80 percent of all business start-ups do not survive beyond the second year. Many fail because they do not have a written business plan.

> *"Know what you know and know what you don't know. Every plan is based on a mixture of known facts, unknowns, and assumptions. Many assumptions can be turned into facts with a little research."*
>
> GENERAL GEORGE S. PATTON

One of the advantages of writing it down is that it forces you to think clearly. For example, the business plan may reveal that you will need to start smaller than you originally thought.

Pray regularly when developing the business plan. Remember, God is the owner of the business, and you are its steward. Ask the Lord for His insight. This is the most important thing you can do. The Bible says, *"I [the Lord] will instruct you and teach you in the way you should go; I will counsel you and watch over you."*[4] One of God's names is *"Wonderful Counselor."*[5] Pray. Take advantage of His willingness to offer you direction.

Address these issues when you create a business plan:

- *Funding:* Determine how you will finance the start-up costs of the business—inventory, equipment, buildings, advertising, etc.
- *Organization:* Choose between a sole proprietorship, a partnership, or a corporation.
- *Marketing:* Identify your competition and determine how you will promote the business.
- *Employees:* Decide how many and what skills they will need.
- *Financial projections:* Estimate your income and expenses.

When it comes to planning, gather all the facts you can. Good planning is always based on accurate information, and that takes work.

World War II military leader General George S. Patton constantly preached to his soldiers about gathering facts. When reviewing the reasons for his commanders' recommendations, he would frequently ask, "How do you know that?"

One of the general's principles was, "Know what you know and know what you don't know. Every plan is based on a mixture of known facts, unknowns, and assumptions. Many assumptions can be turned into facts with a little research."[6]

5. Set up your accounting.

Many start-up businesses fail to keep accurate accounting records. This is dangerous because you will be unable to track your profitability and tax liabilities.

I recommend using a business checking account for depositing all business income and paying all expenses. Record a description of every transaction in a check register or an accounting software program. At the end of an accounting period, it will be easier to compute the profit or loss.

If you are self-employed, a good rule of thumb is to set aside about 30 percent of your net income for taxes and withholding so you won't be forced to use debt to fund your tax payments.

BUSINESS PARTNERSHIPS

Most business partnerships are formed out of economic necessity. Someone has a good idea or time and energy to spend in a business, and someone else has the money to start it.

The Bible cautions us against partnership with those who do not know Christ as Savior. *"Do not be bound together with unbelievers; for what partnership have righteousness and lawlessness, or what fellowship has light with darkness? Or . . . what has a believer in common with an unbeliever?"*[7] The logic behind this is to avoid conflicting values that may lead to compromise in applying God's principles to the business.

I recommend that you *be extremely careful before entering into any partnership—even with someone who knows Christ.* Be sure you know your potential partner very well and, preferably, for a long time. Then answer these questions:

- Does this person have unquestioned integrity and commitment to Christ?
- Does this person consistently handle money according to God's principles?

• If this person is married, is the spouse in favor of the partnership?

Put it in writing—always.

Unraveling a partnership can be heart wrenching. If you reach agreement to form one, write down every detail. It has been said that most of us will retain only 10 percent of what we hear after a month. Combine that with the fact that one person will often misunderstand what another says, and it is easy to see why so many business partners have difficulty sorting out their verbal agreements later.

Address these issues in your written partnership agreement:

• Who will be in charge?
• Will we use debt?
• What happens if we lose money and need more capital?
• How many hours per week will we work in the business?
• How much travel time away from home will we spend?
• Will we give to God's work from the business? If so, how much and to whom?
• What happens if one of us wants to exit the partnership?
• Will we sell the business at some future date?

Remember, the prospects for business success improve tremendously if you save an adequate amount to start it and do your homework by developing a well-thought-through business plan.

Roadside Assistance—Online!

Need to develop a *detailed business plan?* Print an outline of one at **Crown MoneyMap.org**.

Join a small group of business people to encourage one another to operate your businesses God's way. Log on to www.Christatwork.com to learn more.

PART 4 MAKING PROGRESS ON THE JOURNEY

I got my first department store credit card at age seventeen. By the time I graduated from college, I was carrying several cards, a habit I continued into marriage at the age of thirty-four.

My groom, Gaylyn, had also been a career-minded single. But he had never learned the art of living on credit until I, the queen of credit cards, taught him to be the king. In spite of our strong income, we only made the minimum payments.

As the family bookkeeper, I bore the load of managing payments on fifteen cards as well as all of the other monthly payments. It was an organizational nightmare. Even though cash flow was never a problem for us, we weren't prepared for any kind of emergency. I told Gaylyn that if one of us lost a job, we'd have to live with friends or family.

Three years into our marriage, Crown's radio program finally convinced me of the importance of eliminating debt. We had always tithed, but we weren't being faithful in the areas of credit and saving. We needed to make a serious assault on Destination 2 by snowballing our debt.

Over the next four years, we paid off small debts and then applied the monthly payments on those debts to pay off larger ones until we had eliminated them all—to the tune of $65,814. We had to remind each other constantly of one of the memory verses in Crown's small group study: *"Steady plodding brings prosperity; hasty speculation brings poverty"* (Proverbs 21:5 TLB).

Too many people believe they can continue spending and that their jobs will go on forever. Since God has enabled us to escape that trap, we've been excited to lead Crown small groups and help others realize the dangers of debt and the safety of saving.

—JO LYNN AND GAYLYN BRIGHT, *Wichita, Kansas*

Read and watch more stories along the journey at CrownMoneyMap.org.

4 DISCUSSION QUESTIONS

1. Without disclosing any amounts to the group, describe the kinds of consumer debts you have. Have you been successful at paying them off in the past? If not, what is your new plan to eradicate them?

2. If you have had difficulties with creditors, how have you handled them? What, if anything, do you need to change in your communication with them?

3. List your priorities for Destination 4—saving for major purchases. Describe how you will allocate monthly funds for each priority.

4. How can you maximize the principle of compounding? What are you currently doing and what should you change to take full advantage of compounding?

5. If you own a business with indebtedness, what is your plan to pay it off?

6. If you plan to own a business in the future, what are you doing to prepare yourself to start it? What else do you need to do?

4 TOOLS FOR YOUR JOURNEY

• *Christ@Work* (Christatwork.com) is an outstanding organization that has developed practical materials to help you operate a business God's way.

• *Business By the Book*, by Larry Burkett, (Nashville: Nelson, 1998). A superb book on biblical business principles that tens of thousands of businesspeople have applied successfully.

• *Business By the Book Small Group Study*, Crown Financial Ministries. This eight lesson small group study offers in-depth teaching of God's business principles through Bible study, real-life case studies, and interaction with others in your group.

• *Business By the Book Workshop*, Crown Financial Ministries. This six lesson DVD study is designed for individual or group study.

PART

5

DESTINATIONS 5 *and* 6

The grass will feel different under your feet when you own your home—mortgage free.

— DAVE RAMSEY

Author

CHAPTER 17

DESTINATION 5:
BUYING YOUR HOME AND PAYING IT OFF

Jennifer sent Bev an e-mail asking for advice. She was concerned that her brother, John, was about to buy a home that was too expensive for him.

Bev called Jennifer. "Tell me more. What's your brother's income, and how much does this house cost?"

"Well, John's got a good job and earns a reasonable salary," Jennifer answered, "but I think this house is way too much for him. He's single and has been renting an apartment for a few years.

"The good news is that we gave him a copy of the Crown Money Map shortly after we started with it. He's made great progress, paying off all his debts, building his emergency savings, and then saving for the down payment on a house. The problem is that he's fallen in love with a house that costs a fortune."

AFFORDABLE HOUSING

Once you have saved enough for a reasonable down payment (20 percent or more) for the purchase of your home, you are ready to focus on reaching Destination 5. This includes buying an affordable home, beginning to invest, and prepaying the home mortgage.

Our experience with tens of thousands of home buyers has led us to define an *affordable* home:

*Your total housing expenses should not exceed
40 percent of your gross income.*

That 40 percent includes *all* housing expenses: mortgage payment, real estate taxes, utilities, insurance, and maintenance (estimate maintenance each year to be 1–2 percent of the value of the home). If these combined expenses exceed 40 percent of your income, you will need to reduce spending in other categories.

Finding an affordable home is particularly challenging in areas where the cost of housing is extremely expensive. If you are in this situation, there are only three things you can do: *save, pray, and wait.* Save for the down payment; ask the Lord to provide you with an opportunity to buy an affordable home; wait and continue to rent until He does.

Many honest lenders will tell you exactly what you can and cannot afford to borrow. Others care more about their compensation. Since many work on a commission, their motivation is to close the deal. They might qualify you for a loan that is too expensive. So be careful not exceed the guideline of 40 percent of income for all housing expenses.

Prepaying the House Mortgage

A few weeks earlier, we had a discussion with Matt and Jennifer over a disagreement they could not resolve. "I like the tax advantage of the mortgage payment," Matt began, "and I really don't want to prepay the mortgage and decrease the interest payments. Our interest is one of our biggest tax deductions. But Jennifer says we should try to pay off the mortgage. What do you think?"

I explained, "The tax advantage is often misunderstood and overrated.

If you are in the 25 percent tax bracket, for each $1,000 you pay in home mortgage interest, you save $250 in taxes—25 percent of the $1,000 interest paid. So while there is a tax benefit, it's not as much as you may think. Paying $1,000 to save $250 is not *that* great a deal."

"Well," Matt interrupted, "I'd also rather invest the money and earn a greater return than the interest we pay on our mortgage."

"Sure," I responded, "That makes a lot of sense. There's just one catch—there's no such thing as a sure thing in investing. Here's my advice: *do both.* Allocate some of your monthly surplus to investing and some to accelerating the payment of your mortgage."

Matt nodded his head, "That sounds like a reasonable approach." Jennifer agreed.

> **HeyHoward@Crown.org**
>
> **QUESTION:** *I don't think I should pay off my home mortgage because I'd lose the tax advantage of the mortgage payment. What do you think?*
>
> **ANSWER:** *Mortgage interest is tax deductible, but the advantage is overrated. Pay off the mortgage!*

The Goal: A Free and Clear Home

When Bev and I first learned God's financial principles as a young married couple, we asked ourselves if we should pay off our mortgage. We became convinced that God wanted us entirely out of debt, even our home. We understood this to be a *really* long-term goal because of the size of our mortgage and our other debts. But we also knew that the Bible says, *"Steady plodding brings prosperity."*[1] So we committed to be "steady plodders," trusting God to multiply our efforts.

How would it feel to have no debt and no payments of any kind including your home mortgage?

Bev and I realized that if we could pay off our home mortgage, our cost of living would be much lower. It was our largest expense. It would free up a big part of our income so we could give more generously to the work of Christ *and* invest more aggressively to reach our goal of *true financial freedom.*

Without a mortgage, we would enjoy greater financial stability. We could better cope with the cost of a serious illness, loss of a job, or other unexpected financial emergencies. And it would allow Bev to do something she really wanted to do: stay at home and raise our young children.

We did not start prepaying the home mortgage until we wiped out all our credit card and consumer debt. Then we focused on the home. The first step was to understand the numbers.

Understanding the Home Payment Schedule

Every mortgage comes with a payment schedule (also called an amortization schedule) based on the length of the loan and the interest rate. Knowing how this works will help you develop a plan for paying off the mortgage. Let's examine the payment schedule of a mortgage.

Please do not let the mortgage size or the interest rate in this illustration hinder your thinking. In the example below, we are assuming a $150,000 mortgage at a 7.5 percent fixed interest rate, paid over thirty years. The first year looks like this:

STARTLING STATS:

During the first several years of a thirty-year mortgage, your payments are almost all interest. In fact, it will be twenty-three years before the principal and interest portions of the monthly payment equal each other!

PAYMENT SCHEDULE FOR A THIRTY-YEAR MORTGAGE
(at 7.5 percent)

Paymt.#	Month	Payment	Interest	Principal	Balance
0					150,000.00
1	Jan	1,048.82	937.50	111.32	149,888.68
2	Feb	1,048.82	936.80	112.02	149,776.66
3	Mar	1,048.82	936.10	112.72	149,663.94
4	Apr	1,048.82	935.40	113.42	149,550.52
5	May	1,048.82	934.69	114.13	149,436.39
6	Jun	1,048.82	933.98	114.84	149,321.55
7	Jul	1,048.82	933.26	115.56	149,205.98
8	Aug	1,048.82	932.54	116.28	149,089.70

9	Sep	1,048.82	931.81	117.01	148,972.69
10	Oct	1,048.82	931.08	117.74	148,854.95
11	Nov	1,048.82	930.34	118.48	148,736.47
12	Dec	1,048.82	929.60	119.22	148,617.25

Totals for year:	12,585.84	11,203.11	1,382.73

As you can see, the payments during the first year are largely interest. Of the $12,585.84 in payments, only $1,382.73 will go toward principal reduction. In fact, it will be twenty-three years before the principal and interest portions of the payment will equal each other!

Now here's something really important to remember. *Interest is charged on the remaining unpaid principal balance.* Look at the schedule above.

In January, if you paid your first monthly payment of $1,048.82 *plus* the next month's principal payment of $112.02, the principal balance would be $149,776.66. So in February when you make your regular payment of $1,048.82, it is applied as though it were payment #3. Now, look carefully at payment #2. You paid $112.02 extra and saved the $936.80 in interest you would have paid. That is a great deal! Can you see why I hope that you will catch the vision of paying off your home? There's nothing magical about what I'm suggesting. Once you understand how it works, the numbers will work *for* you.

HOW TO PAY OFF THE MORTGAGE MORE QUICKLY

I don't know about you, but a thirty-year goal to pay off my home mortgage doesn't excite me—it seems like forever. But if I can shorten it, the goal is much more attainable. There are several ways to accelerate the payment of your home mortgage.

1. Reduce the length of the mortgage.

If you need a new mortgage or the conditions are favorable for you to refinance, consider a shorter-term mortgage. If you can afford higher payments, go with a fifteen-year instead of a thirty-year mortgage. The interest rate on a fifteen-year mortgage is normally lower than the thirty-year rate, and the outstanding balance shrinks much faster.

Let's compare a $150,000, thirty-year mortgage at 7.5 percent and a fifteen-year mortgage at 7 percent.

Total Mortgage $150,000	Thirty Years	Fifteen Years
Monthly Payment	$ 1,048	$ 1,348
At the end of fifteen years:		
Interest paid	$ 151,928	$ 92,683
Principal paid	$ 36,859	$ 150,000
Principal balance due	$ 131,140	$ 0 (Yes!)
Interest paid, years 15–30	$ 75,649	$ 0
Total Interest Paid	$ 227,577	$ 92,683

If you can shrink the duration of your mortgage in half, the savings in interest is huge.

Here's the key question for you to answer: Can I afford the larger monthly payment? If it will put too much strain on your budget or will not allow you to meet your other financial goals, then I recommend a longer mortgage with a lower monthly payment.

2. Add something to the required payment.

You can still accelerate the repayment of your mortgage simply by paying an extra amount each month or as frequently as possible.

That's what Bev and I did. We started small. Each month we put a little more on the mortgage to reduce the principal more quickly. The longer we did it, the more excited we became.

One simple method of prepaying is to set up an automatic withdrawal from your checking account each month. This is an easy way to manage and keep track of your monthly payments.

3. Bonuses and tax returns.

Finally, when you receive a work bonus or an income tax refund, give generously to the Lord and then consider applying the rest to your home mortgage. Doing that each time it occurs can have a significant impact on paying off your home.

I remember receiving an unexpected bonus. Instead of taking a vacation or buying something nice but unnecessary, Bev and I applied those dollars toward the mortgage. Because the funds went directly against the principal, that bonus alone allowed us to shorten our mortgage by several years.

TIME TO GET PRACTICAL

Once you have decided to pay off your home, take these steps to make certain your mortgage and your lender line up with the plan:

1. Let your lender know what you are planning. Not many borrowers prepay their mortgages, so the lender may be in shock for a while!

2. If you pay by check, write one for your regular payment and a separate check for the amount of principal you are prepaying. Note on the check that it is to be applied *only* toward prepaying the principle. That creates a paper trail should there ever be a question of your prepayment history. If you pay electronically, keep a copy of your monthly bank statements.

3. Get a payment schedule (amortization schedule) for your mortgage and track your progress every month. This is very important. You'll be enormously encouraged as you see the balance reducing. Remember, paying off your home mortgage usually takes years, and you'll need lots of encouragement to stay at it.

4. Once a year, contact your lender to confirm the unpaid balance of the

What would happen if you became completely debt-free and you began to invest what you had been making in monthly payments?

mortgage. Do that to make certain the lender is properly crediting your prepayments.

REFINANCING YOUR MORTGAGE

When interest rates drop, it may be wise to consider refinancing your mortgage at a lower interest rate. As a rule of thumb, refinancing makes sense when you can pay for its costs within two to three years through what you save each month because of the lower interest rate.

Sadly, many people use the refinance option to increase the amount of house debt and spend the cash they take out. If you refinance, use this opportunity to reduce the number of years left on your mortgage. For example, if you can reduce its length from thirty years to twenty while still making about the same monthly payment, do it!

Interest rates may be fixed or adjustable. A fixed-rate mortgage charges the same rate of interest during the life of the mortgage. The advantage of the fixed rate is that your payment is predictable. There is less risk because during a period of rising interest rates, your monthly payment doesn't go up.

An adjustable-rate mortgage, commonly called an ARM, periodically adjusts its rate to reflect the current market. The two advantages of an ARM are that the initial rate is usually lower than a fixed rate, and if rates go down, so does your monthly payment. However when rates escalate, an ARM can devastate your finances.

Consider an adjustable rate mortgage if you plan on staying in your home seven years or less *and* the government is trying to help economic growth by reducing interest rates. Otherwise, stick with a fixed rate mortgage.

MORTGAGES TO AVOID
Biweekly Payments

A biweekly payment means that you pay half of the monthly payment every two weeks. Many consumers receive biweekly payment offers—usually laced with deception. Most of the offers come through companies that charge for this service. Making twenty-six biweekly payments a year is simply the equivalent of making thirteen monthly payments instead of twelve. You can make one extra monthly payment a year or add one-twelfth of a payment each month and save the fee! Take my advice: Don't use a biweekly payment plan to prepay your mortgage.

Interest-Only Mortgages

Interest-only mortgages have become increasingly popular. Because no portion of the payment goes toward principal, the payments are lower and customers are able to qualify for a more expensive house.

They are *very* dangerous. Since there is no reduction of principal, if the home drops in value, the loan balance will be greater than the value of the home. If the rate on the interest-only mortgage is adjustable, then payments can increase—sometimes significantly.

The bottom line: Don't be tempted by interest-only mortgages. They are far too dangerous.

MORTGAGE INSURANCE: WHAT YOU SHOULD KNOW

If you buy a home loan with less than a 20 percent down payment, your lender probably will require you to buy mortgage insurance (PMI) to protect *their* interests in case you default. Mortgage insurance is expensive. The monthly cost is about $45 for every $100,000 of the original mortgage amount.

Once the equity in your home reaches 20 percent, you can stop carrying mortgage insurance unless you have an FHA loan, which requires premium payments for the life of the loan. You can eliminate mortgage insurance sooner if you prepay on the loan and build your equity faster. Also, if your home has appreciated significantly, some lenders will consider a new appraisal instead of the original one when deciding if you've met the 20 percent equity threshold.

BEV GETS BEHIND THE WHEEL

What's it like owning your own home free and clear? Bev shares her experience: "The idea of owning our home mortgage-free appealed to me. Howard and I knew it wasn't going to happen overnight, and it didn't. But we paid off the mortgage faster than we initially hoped because God provided additional funds for us in an unexpected way.

"When we paid the last mortgage payment, I was surprised to feel a wonderful sense of freedom and relief. I realized that if Howard would die before my children went out on their own, I would be able to continue raising them in our home. That was a huge source of comfort.

"I believe that the Lord wants us totally free from debt—even our homes. So, if you own a home, I encourage you to seek the Lord and learn whether He would have you begin paying off the mortgage. If He leads you to do it, He will also provide the way

Roadside Assistance—Online!

Mortgage calculator. Want to print your own home mortgage payment schedule? Want to find out how much you can shorten your mortgage and save by making extra payments? Want to compare mortgages and interest rates? Log on to **CrownMoneyMap.org** for calculators and links.

Steady plodding brings prosperity;
hasty speculation brings poverty.
— KING SOLOMON

CHAPTER 18

DESTINATION 5:

INVESTING

"We don't know even where to begin," said Jennifer nervously. "We realize that we're in way over our heads."

"She's right," nodded Matt. "We've reached Destination 5 and now we're supposed to start investing, but we have no experience. Our next-door neighbors just lost thousands of dollars investing in what they thought was a sure thing. We don't know who to trust."

"Investing can be confusing, but you can trust the Bible," I responded, smiling. "It contains very practical investing advice. But before we take a look at what it says about investing, we need to be aware of two important principles."

FINDING THE BALANCE: INVESTING AND GIVING

We need to balance our investing with generosity. Jesus told a parable of a farmer who harvested a bumper crop and said to himself, "*I have no place to store my crops. . . . I will tear down my barns and build bigger ones, and there I will store* ***all*** *my grain and my goods. . . .' But God said to him, 'You fool! . . . This is how it* *will be with anyone who stores up things for himself but is not rich toward God. . . . For where your treasure is, there your heart will be also.'"*[1]

> We need to balance our investing with generosity because *"where your treasure is, there your heart will be also."*

The key word in this parable is *all.* Jesus called the farmer foolish because he saved everything. He did not *balance* saving with generous giving. If we only pile up our investments, those assets will pull on our hearts like gravity. Our affection will be drawn away from God toward them, because *"where your treasure is, there your heart will be also."* However, if we give generously to God, we can invest *and* still love Him with all of our heart.

A DANGEROUS DESIRE

Let's face it—most people want to get rich. I'll never forget how surprised I was the first time I realized the Bible's strong caution *against* it: *"People who want to get rich fall into temptation and a trap and into many foolish and harmful desires that plunge men into ruin and destruction."*[2] Read this verse again. It says those who want to get rich give in to temptations and desires that ultimately lead to ruin. Wanting to get rich is incredibly dangerous, but why?

The next verse answers that question: *"For the love of money is a root of all kinds of evil. Some people, eager for money, have wandered from the faith and pierced themselves with many griefs."*[3] When we want to get rich, we actually *love* money. That has consequences I have witnessed firsthand. Mike, a close friend, became consumed by a desire to get rich. He finally abandoned his wife and four young sons and later denied Christ.

For much of my life I wanted to become rich—not just a little rich— filthy rich! So dealing with this attitude has been difficult. Here is what I discovered: When I wanted to get rich, my motivations were pride, greed, or an urge to prepare for survival in uncertain economic times. I loved *money.* However, when I desired to be a faithful steward and invest wisely the money God entrusted to me, my motive completely changed. I simply wanted to please Him. I loved *God.*

Understand, I am *not* saying it is wrong to become rich. In the Bible, many heroes of the faith, such as Abraham and David, were rich.[4] In fact, I rejoice when God enables a person who has been an ambitious, faithful steward to prosper. *Nothing is wrong with becoming wealthy if it is a by-product of being faithful.*

GOD'S PRINCIPLES OF INVESTING

This chapter is not intended to address everything you need to know about investing. Visit CrownMoneyMap.org for more helpful information. The Bible provides us with four basic guidelines for investing.

1. Be a steady plodder.

The fundamental principle for becoming a successful investor is to spend less than you earn and then regularly invest the surplus. In other words, be a steady plodder. We've talked about this before. The Bible says, *"Steady plodding brings prosperity hasty speculation brings poverty."*[5] The original words for "steady plodding" picture a person filling a large barrel one handful at a time. Little by little the barrel is filled to overflowing. Nothing replaces consistent, month after month investing. Regardless of the economy or investment climate— just do it.

2. Seek advice.

Each of us has limited knowledge and experience. God encourages us to seek counsel to secure suggestions from others that will aid in making good decisions: *"Listen to advice and accept instruction, and in the end you will be wise."*[6] This is especially true when making investment decisions.

- *Seek the advice of a professional.* If you are not an experienced investor, I recommend that you use a financial planner or investment advisor when you reach Destination 5 and begin investing. It is crucial to use an advisor who understands what the *Bible* says about money because it will make a huge difference in the quality of their advice. If you do not know one, Christian Financial Professionals Network (CFPN.org) is an excellent place to search. I suggest interviewing at least three candidates before choosing the one with whom you are most comfortable.

- *Seek the advice of your spouse.* If you are married, the first person you should consult is your spouse. Unfortunately, I didn't do this when I was younger. Bev had no formal financial training, and I assumed she would be little help making investment decisions. I was so wrong! Over the years her advice has been superb and has saved us "big bucks."

> **HeyHoward@Crown.org**
>
> **QUESTION:** *I like investing in high-risk, high-return investments. Unfortunately, my wife doesn't feel comfortable with my approach. How can I convince her I'm right?*
> **ANSWER:** *Listen to her advice! God speaks most clearly to the husband through his wife.*

A few more words on seeking counsel from your spouse. In marriage, the man and the woman complement each other; their strengths compensate for each other's weaknesses. Women tend to be gifted with an extraordinarily accurate intuitive sense. Men tend to focus objectively on the facts. A husband and wife need each other to achieve the proper balance for a correct decision.

I believe that God honors the wife's office as *"helper"*[7] to her husband. Many times the Lord communicates most clearly to a man through his wife. And as long as you agree on a decision, even if it proves to be wrong, there are no grounds for an "I told you so" fracture in your relationship.

3. Diversify.

No investment is guaranteed, and money can be lost on any of them. The stock market, bonds, real estate, gold—you name it—can perform well or poorly. Each type of investment has its own advantages and disadvantages. Since the perfect investment doesn't exist, we need to diversify and not put all our eggs in one basket. The Bible says, *"Divide your portion to seven, or even to eight, for you do not know what misfortune may occur on the earth."*[8]

4. Limit investment debt.

In my opinion, it is permissible to borrow for an investment, if the invest-ment (along with your down payment) is the sole collateral for the debt. You should not personally guarantee repayment of the debt. At first, this may appear to contradict the Bible's instruction to repay our debts: *"The wicked borrows and does not pay back."*[9] But let's explore this further.

Suppose you wanted to purchase a rental property, and you asked the seller to carry the mortgage. You offer a reasonable down payment and stipu-late that the house be the sole security for the debt. You explain to the seller that at your option you will repay the loan in one of two ways: First, by giving the seller cash—making all the payments. Or second, by giving the seller the property back along with the down payment and any other money you have invested in the house.

Given those options, the seller must make a decision. Is the down pay-ment sufficient? Is the real estate market strong enough for the seller to feel secure about making the loan?

Because of the possibility of difficult financial events over which you have no control, be sure to limit your potential loss to the cash you invest and the asset itself. It is painful to lose your investment, but it is much more serious to jeopardize all your assets on investment debt. What I'm suggesting may appear too conservative, but many people have lost everything by guar-anteeing debt on investments that went sour.

APPLYING THE PRINCIPLES: WHEN AND WHERE TO INVEST

Now let's apply those four biblical investing principles.

When deciding where to invest, you need to consider your goals, time frame and personal tolerance to risk. The concept of risk is important because, as the "Time & Risk" diagram (next page) shows, investments with the greatest track record of growth also carry the greatest potential for loss—at least in the short run.

In other words, the more time you have, the more you can afford to invest in stocks, mutual funds, or real estate—all investments that can lose value in the short term but historically offer the best growth opportunity over the long term. If you have five, ten, or twenty years before you need the money, you can probably recover from most market downturns, but if you need it in less than five, you should alter your approach.

This means using different investments for different goals. An investment that is suitable for a fifteen-year goal is simply not appropriate for money you will need in two years. If you need the down payment to buy your home in two years as opposed to funding your retirement in fifteen years, you will invest the money differently. Move your money into more conservative investments as you get closer to the time you will need to spend it.

With that in mind, here are specific strategies to consider over the short (less than five years) and long (more than five years) term.

Time & Risk

Shorter	TIME FRAME	Longer
CASH-EQUIVALENT	**BONDS**	**STOCKS / REAL ESTATE**
Investments easily converted to cash	Issued by a borrower seeking to raise funds	Ownership of company shares / Real Estate
• *Money Market Funds* • *Short-Term Certificates of Deposit* • *Treasury Bills*	• *Bond Mutual Funds* • *Government Bonds* • *Corporate Bonds*	• *Stock Mutual Funds* • *Individual Stocks* • *Real Estate*
Lower	RISK & RETURN	**Higher**

Less Than Five Years

When you need the money in less than five years, invest in what are known as cash equivalents: *money market funds, short-term certificates of deposit (CDs),* and

Treasury bills (T-bills). Your five-year investment portfolio would look like this:

Money market funds can be purchased through brokerage firms and banks. They usually earn more than regular bank accounts and can have check writing privileges. *Short-term CDs,* issued by banks, typically mature in lengths from three months to five years. If the bank issuing the CD is federally insured, your money is insured up to $100,000. *T-bills* are backed by the federal government and are free from state taxes. They mature in three to twelve months.

All Cash Equivalents

Longer Than Five Years

The most common investments of longer than five years are *mutual funds, stocks, bonds,* and *real estate.*

Mutual funds. There are more than eight-thousand mutual funds from which to choose, and the biggest advantage of investing in them is that you can apply the biblical principles of diversification and professional investment advice. Mutual funds receive money from investors, and they in turn invest in dozens or even hundreds of other companies. Mutual fund managers hire professional analysts who carefully study the companies in which they might invest. They know a lot more about them than the average person, and they select the companies that they believe will provide the best return for their investors.

There are many kinds of mutual funds. Some are composed of stocks, some of bonds; some contain both. Others mutual funds consist of international stocks or are limited in their selection to a particular sector, such as real estate. There are also many types of bond funds—those invested in government bonds, corporate bonds, or tax-free municipal bonds. A *balanced mutual fund* invests in cash-equivalents, stocks, and bonds. All mutual funds are sold with a written prospectus that describes the *fund objective* that tells you how your money will be invested.

Choose funds that have solid track records for a minimum of five years; ten years is even better. There are excellent mutual funds that have averaged 10 to 12 percent annual returns and keep their expenses low.

Almost anyone can invest in a mutual fund. Some funds will accept as little as $500 to open an account and allow monthly investments as small as $50.

Stocks. When you buy a stock, you are purchasing part of a company. Generally, stock ownership has one of the greatest opportunities for profit, but you also can lose a lot if the company does not perform well. Some stocks pay an income called a dividend.

Bonds. When you buy a bond, you *loan* money to a business or the government, and they pay you interest. Generally, high-quality bonds are less risky than stocks. Investors buy government bonds for safety, municipal bonds for tax-free returns, and corporate bonds for higher yields. It is important to realize that when interest rates rise, the value of bonds decline, and vice versa.

Real estate. People buy rental property for income or unimproved property for appreciation. There are tax advantages for owning buildings because depreciation is deductible. However, unlike publicly traded stocks or bonds that can be sold quickly, real estate may require a long time to sell. A major downside of rental property can be the time, money, and effort required to rent, manage, and maintain it.

Investment Road Map

I have developed a mini Road Map with three of its own destinations for investing. The strategy is to start conservatively and raise the percentage of higher risk/higher reward investments as the total investment amount grows. Always maintain a foundation of conservative assets as a stable base upon which to build higher-growth-potential assets. If you are a savvy investor or have expertise in an area of investing, you will need to factor that in your personal strategy.

I have found it wise to keep 25 percent of investments in cash-equivalents. Occasionally, I will become aware of an unusually good opportunity and am able to invest in it because of the cash. Then I replenish the cash-equivalents as soon as practical.

Investing Destination 1	**Investing Destination 2**	**Investing Destination 3**
Amount: Under $10,000	**Amount:** $10,000 to $50,000	**Amount:** More than $50,000
Mix: Balanced mutual funds & conservative stocks, bonds (75%)	**Mix:** Balanced mutual funds & conservative stocks, bonds (50%)	**Mix:** Balanced mutual fund and conservative stocks, bonds (25%)
Cash-equivalents (25%)	Higher-risk mutual funds and stocks, bonds (25%)	Higher-risk mutual funds and stocks, bonds (25%)
	Cash-equivalents (25%)	Cash-equivalents (25%)
		Real estate & other investments (25%)

Remember, the name of the game at Destination 5 is to be a *steady plodder*. As consistently as possible, add to your investments and allow them to compound.

APPLYING THE PRINCIPLES: THINK TAXES

Taxes also can influence your investment decisions. *Long-term capital gains* are taxed at lower rates than ordinary income. Under current tax law, if you hold an investment for at least a year and then sell it for a profit, the profit will be taxed at the favorable long-term capital gains rate.

Tax-free municipal bonds generally pay a lower rate of return than taxable investments but may yield a better after-tax return. To determine which pays the most after taxes, use this formula:

Taxable return x (100% - your tax bracket) = comparable tax-free return

Assume you pay combined federal and state taxes of 25 percent, and you are trying to decide between buying a municipal bond that pays 5 percent and a taxable bond that pays 7 percent. The formula would look like this:

$$7\% \times (100\% - 25\%) = .07 \times .75 = 5.25\%$$

The municipal bond would need to return 5.25 percent to equal the taxable 7 percent return for someone in the 25 percent tax bracket.

APPLYING THE PRINCIPLES: AVOID RISKY INVESTMENTS

God warns us to avoid risky investments, yet each year thousands of people lose money in highly speculative investments and scams. The Bible says, *"There is another serious problem I have seen everywhere—savings are put into risky investments that turn sour, and soon there is nothing left to pass on to one's son. The man who speculates is soon back to where he began—with nothing."*[10]

How many times have you heard of people losing their life's savings on a get-rich-quick scheme? Sadly, it seems that Christians are particularly vulnerable because they trust others who appear to live by their same values.

These characteristics will help you identify a risky investment:

- It will practically guarantee an unusually high profit or rate of return.
- It requires a quick decision with little or no opportunity to investigate the investment or its promoter.
- It will say little or nothing about the risks of losing money.

The strategy for avoiding risky investments is to pray, seek wise counsel, and do your homework.

APPLYING THE PRINCIPLES: GAMBLING AND LOTTERIES

"I know that gambling isn't exactly like investing," Matt said. "But one of the salesmen at work is really hooked on it. What does the Bible say about gambling?"

Lotteries and gambling of all types are sweeping our country. Internet gambling is exploding. Each year one in four Americans gambles at a casino.

The average church member gives $20 a year to international missions while the average person gambles $1,174 annually.[11]

Sadly, more than six million Americans are addicted to gambling, with consequences that are heartbreaking for their loved ones. Although the Bible does not specifically prohibit gambling, its *get-rich-quick* motivation violates the steady plodding principle.

In my opinion, we should *never* participate in gambling or lotteries—even for entertainment. We should not expose ourselves to the risk of becoming compulsive gamblers, nor should we support an industry that enslaves so many.

Roadside Assistance—Online!

For more on *investing*, visit **CrownMoneyMap.org**.

This is what the Lord says: "Put your house in order, because you are going to die."

—THE PROPHET ISAIAH

The younger generation must develop financial wisdom before they can manage financial wealth.

— RON BLUE

Author of Splitting Heirs

DESTINATION 6:

PLANNING YOUR ESTATE

"To be honest, we feel a little guilty," Matt said looking down at the ground. "We're making great progress getting to Destination 6. It won't be too much longer until our home is paid off."

"And we'll soon have saved what we want to contribute to our children's college education," added Jennifer. "But that's not what Matt's feeling guilty about. It's the will and estate planning we've been putting off."

"That's right," confessed Matt. "We haven't wanted to think about preparing for our deaths."

"I understand," I said. "But God wants you to be faithful stewards—in life *and* death. If you die without a will, the state decides how to distribute your assets and even who will be the guardian of your children. These are decisions I know you want to make."

Let's remind ourselves of two realities:

- *We all will die. "This is what the Lord says: 'Put your house in order, because you are going to die. '"*[1]

- *We will take nothing with us.* After wealthy John D. Rockefeller died, his accountant was asked how much he left. The accountant responded, "He left it all." The apostle Paul said it this way, *"For we brought nothing into the world, and we can take nothing out of it."* [2]

STARTLING STATS:

Seventy percent of Americans die without a current will.

Estate planning is not merely a financial or legal matter; it is a spiritual exercise we work out in God's presence and for His glory. What a fantastic privilege God has granted us to select the next stewards of our assets.

Looking at the big picture, you have only three choices for who will receive your estate:

Stu's Views   © 2003 Stu All Rights Reserved www.STUS.com

I take it this will is contested.

1. *Your heirs.*
2. *Non-profit organizations.* Although tax savings is not the primary goal, transferring assets to a church or ministry is the most tax-efficient choice. Gifts to non-profits are 100 percent deductible from your estate. I strongly recommend that you honor God by leaving something to His work.
3. *Government.* Many people unintentionally make the government a beneficiary by paying estate taxes they could have avoided or reduced through wise tax planning.

PROVIDING FOR YOUR HEIRS

The Bible says parents should try to leave an inheritance to their children. *"A good man leaves an inheritance to his children's children."* [3] However, if you are unable to do so, do not feel guilty. You can only do what you can do. Consider these three action steps to help ensure that the inheritance you leave for your children and grandchildren will be a blessing.

Train them.

The younger generation must develop financial wisdom *before* they can manage wealth. The inheritance should not be distributed until they have been trained to be good money managers. *"An inheritance gained hurriedly at the beginning will not be blessed in the end."*[4] In the next chapter, I'll talk about teaching children how to handle money God's way.

> *Children must develop financial wisdom before they can manage wealth.*

Decide when.

If your heirs are young, I suggest that you consider spreading their inheritance over several years. Our children are to receive certain percentages of the inheritance when they turn twenty-one, thirty, and thirty-five. As they mature, it is our hope they will learn from any mistakes and become wiser with their money. We selected trustworthy people to help supervise their finances until they reach thirty-five. *"As long as the heir is a child, he is no different from a slave, although he owns the whole estate. He is subject to guardians and trustees until the time set by his father."*[5]

Decide how much.

How much should you leave your children and grandchildren? This is a huge issue. Assess how well they have been trained to handle money. Then pray and seek advice. If you are married, discuss this with your spouse.

Thoughtful people have reached a wide variety of conclusions regarding what is most beneficial for the heirs. Some have limited their bequest to cover only the costs of college or vocational training; others have chosen to leave everything.

The amount may differ for each child.

Probably every parent of more than one child has asked this question: How can children coming from the same parents and living in the same environment be so *different*? Then, as children become adults, their values and lifestyles may differ even more.

As you think about leaving children an inheritance, you may realize that some of your children are better equipped to handle possessions than others are. And some have more genuine needs than others. For example, one daughter may have been divorced and left alone to raise four young children. Another daughter may own a profitable business.

We are to love our children equally, which often means helping them uniquely. They are unique in not only their character, values, commitment to Christ, and ability to deal with life but also their vocation, health, and immediate family situation. These circumstances may influence how much you plan to leave each child and, as circumstances change, you may need to adjust your plan accordingly.

> *Few areas have more potential for harming family relationships than squabbles over inheritance.*

Leaving unequal amounts may be a difficult decision because it feels unfair. We simply encourage you to ask for God's guidance if you need to consider such action.

ADDRESSING FAMILY PROBLEMS

Few areas have more potential for harming family relationships than squabbles over inheritance. Someone asked Jesus, *"'Tell my brother to divide the inheritance with me.' Jesus replied . . . 'Watch out! Be on your guard against all kinds of greed.'"* [6] He recognized how easily the receiving of an inheritance can degenerate into greed. A family conference can help overcome this problem.

Many parents are not comfortable discussing inheritance plans with their children. Adult children are even less comfortable bringing it up because they don't want to be perceived as nosy or greedy.

I recommend holding a family conference because it can provide tremendous benefits, including peace of mind. It gives your heirs the opportunity to hear from you—your heart, your wishes. It also gives them the opportunity to ask questions. Although parents still make the distribution decisions, such a meeting promotes open communication while everyone is present rather than after a death—when most family conferences occur.

Parents should wait until their children are old enough to understand the reasons for the meeting. When parents and adult children do not talk about these issues, there is more uncertainty and sometimes more conflict after the parents' death.

> **HeyHoward@Crown.org**
>
> **QUESTION:** *How often should I review my will?*
> **ANSWER:** *Review it every three years—even sooner if you or your family experience significant changes or there is a change in the tax law.*

OTHER INHERITANCE ISSUES
Review of your estate plan

How often should you review your estate plan? Review your plan every three years—perhaps sooner if you or your family experience significant changes. Keep in mind that these plans are not static. As circumstances change—tax laws, giving opportunities, new information—you will want to review your plan.

First things first.

First, decide *how you want to distribute* your assets and *how to prepare* your heirs for what they will receive. Only after you have made these decisions should you engage an attorney experienced in estates to draw up the documents. Doing it the other way around often results in an attorney not understanding what you really want to accomplish. Visit CrownMoneyMap.org for an estate planning worksheet to assist you.

Remember, it is important to prepare for your death. One of the greatest gifts you can leave your loved ones for that emotional time will be an organized estate and a properly prepared will or revocable living trust. If you do not have a current will or trust, please make an appointment to prepare one.[7]

5 MAKING PROGRESS ON THE JOURNEY

How did it come to this? A few years earlier, I was sitting on top of the world. The scholarship I received at age nineteen would pay half my expenses all the way through law school. I decided to start my big-shot life early.

A mountain of student loans and credit cards made the good life easy until one year into law school I was staring at a $100,000 debt load. A few minor legal problems later, my school asked me to leave.

I felt as though I was at the bottom rung of life. My day job only covered the minimum payments on my credit cards, and now I had to find a night job to eat.

A valet job required a uniform, but I couldn't afford $50 for the black tennis shoes. I went to a discount store and found some black ladies' gardening shoes for $5.99. A magic marker darkened the white bands around them—sort of.

One night while parking a car, I turned the radio dial and heard part of Crown's program. It's amazing how God can get your attention, even listening to the radio in someone else's car for just a couple of minutes.

I gave Jesus Christ my heart, and together we began to make big changes. Soon I was at Destination 1 and working toward Destination 2—my massive credit card debt. Then came Destination 3, when four years later I made the last payment on my student loan.

Next, my wife and I saved for four years and made a 50 percent down payment on a house, paying off the mortgage in another four years. We were at Destination 6.

Now a financially free CPA, I know the joy of being a Crown Money Map coach and offering others the hope of an impossible dream.

—**KEVIN CROSS**, *Hollywood, Florida*

Read and watch more stories along the journey at CrownMoneyMap.org.

DISCUSSION QUESTIONS

1. If you own a home, what is your strategy to pay off the mortgage?

2. If you want to own a home, describe what an *affordable* one would look like for you.

3. What were the most important investment principles you learned from reading this section? How will you implement them?

4. How would you describe your investing style (steady plodder, risk taker, other)? In light of learning God's investment principles, do you need to change? In what way?

5. Do you have a current will? If not, what is hindering you from securing one?

6. What was the most challenging concept you studied in this section? Why did it challenge you?

 **TOOLS FOR YOUR JOURNEY**

Financial professionals

Visit the Web site of *Christian Financial Professionals Network* at CFPN.org for a listing of financial professionals who have been trained to handle money God's way.

Mutual Funds

Log on to *SoundMindInvesting.com* to learn about investing in mutual funds from a biblical perspective.

Estate Planning

Splitting Heirs, by author Ron Blue is an outstanding book dealing with estate issues, by Moody Publishers.

Set Your House in Order workbook enables you to collect all the information your heirs will need in one notebook, by Crown Financial Ministries.

PART

6

DESTINATION 7

Train up a child in the way he should go,
and when he is old he will not depart from it.

— KING SOLOMON

20

THIS IS A
FAMILY TRIP!

It had been a long time since Bev and I had watched a basketball game played by third graders.

Matt and Jennifer had invited us to watch their son, Kyle, and it was great fun. By half time, Kyle's team was leading by three points, and he was top scorer with six.

"As you can see, our kids are growing up. And we're, well, we're super concerned about them. All their friends spend money like crazy, and our kids are starting to do the same. We want to make sure they learn to handle money God's way," Jennifer began.

"That's right," Matt affirmed. "We certainly don't want them to make the same mistakes we've made. We're afraid that we are starting too late. What should we do?"

Bev smiled. "I'm so glad you're thinking about that now. Most parents just take this part of their children's education for granted, but the world is pounding them with the wrong messages. You've got to be very intentional with your kids these days.

"By high school graduation, the average student has seen more than a million ads on TV and the Internet. And they're all saying the same thing—spend your money here.

Then Bev mentioned a doll that still amazes her (and me too). "Several years ago, a best-selling doll was named Cool Shoppin'. She carried a credit card, and when it was swiped through a small credit card reader, it said 'credit approved.' This doll was marketed to girls as young as three years old."

"That's right," I added. "It's something for which parents must take responsibility. The Bible says, *'Train up a child in the way he should go, even when he is old he will not depart from it.'*[1] And while the best time to start is when your children are young, it's never too late.

"The consequences of not teaching children to handle money wisely are tragic. So many young adults today are out of control financially. They are drowning in debt with almost no savings, and they don't understand how important it is to be generous."

GRADUATING TO GREATER RESPONSIBILITY

The fundamental strategy for training children to handle money is the *Little-Big* principle. The Bible says, *"He who is faithful in a very little thing is faithful also in much."*[2]

When children become faithful with small amounts, they are prepared to assume greater responsibility. After they learn to handle quarters wisely, they are ready for a few dollars. Parents should be as systematic in equipping children to handle money as teachers are in teaching them to write. First, children learn the alphabet and then how to spell their name. Each year they learn more complex words and grammar. Eventually, they are able to write essays. Learning to handle words—or money—is a process that happens in stages.

The strategy is to steadily increase responsibility so that your children are independently managing all their finances—with the exception of food and shelter—by their senior year in high school. That way, parents are available to watch and advise as their children make increasingly important

216

financial decisions while still at home.

Unfortunately, most young people are unprepared to handle money when they leave home. One college student admitted how shocked he was to learn that credit card purchases actually had to be paid for later! That surprise paled in comparison to how stunned his parents were when they received his credit card statement with an outstanding balance of $11,350!

> **STARTLING STATS:**
>
> The fastest-growing age group filing bankruptcy is twenty to twenty-four. More people of all age groups file for bankruptcy than graduate from college.

By the time your children are in their junior year of high school, they should open a checking account and get a secured credit card. Parents can then show them how to reconcile their checkbook each month, coaching them to use the credit card wisely and pay it off in full and on time every month. Once those habits are in place, they will likely stay in place for a lifetime.

MVPs

Parents should be *MVP Parents*. MVP is an acronym that describes the three methods to teach children God's way of handling money: *Modeling, Verbal communication,* and *Practical opportunities*. All three are needed to train your children. Let's look at each method.

Modeling

Since children soak up parental attitudes toward money like a sponge soaks up water, parents must model handling money God's way. The apostle Paul recognized the importance of modeling when he said, *"Be imitators of me, just as I also am of Christ."* [3] Nothing influences children more than watching parents live out what they believe. That's especially true in the area of finances. Your kids watch how you spend money, pick up on your attitudes toward buying on credit, and observe your patterns of giving and saving. What you do with money must be consistent with what you say about it. Your children are listening *and* watching you.

Verbal Communication

> *"Example is not the main thing in influencing others, it is the only thing."*
>
> Albert Schweitzer

We should verbally instruct our children in the ways of the Lord. The Lord said to His people, *"These words, which I am commanding you today, shall be on your heart. You shall teach them diligently to your sons and shall talk of them when you sit in your house and when you walk by the way and when you lie down and when you rise up."*[4] Look at this passage carefully. Parents are instructed to talk of the truths in the Bible when they are hanging out at home or traveling around, from first thing in the morning until time to go to sleep at night.

Consistently tell your children how God's practical truths apply to their finances. Use natural times, such as when you're grocery shopping or walking through the hardware store or waiting in line at the bank—these are perfect opportunities to instruct your children on the wise use of money.

Practical Opportunities

Give your children opportunities to apply what they have heard and seen. Design these experiences to be appropriate for their age and unique personality. Young children, for example, are not yet able to grasp abstract concepts, so their practical experiences need to be tangible and easy to understand. The more *hands-on* the experience, the more children will learn.

> *The more hands-on the experience, the more children will learn.*

THE GAME PLAN
Learning to Work

Parents should help their children learn the satisfaction of a job well done. Learning to enjoy work and develop proper work habits is a giant step toward becoming productive and valuable in the job market.

The best way for young children to learn to work is to establish daily household chores for each member of the family. For example, my daughter washed the dishes, and my son cleaned the floors.

Also, encourage your children to do extra work to earn money. A good rule of thumb is to pay the child a fair wage for the work you would have to hire someone to do. For example, if your car needs washing and your daughter wants to wash it, let her. Be happy to pay her rather than the man at the car wash.

As children grow older, working for others by mowing lawns, babysitting or waiting on tables is an education that allows them to enter into an employee-employer relationship, learn people skills, and earn extra money.

The objective of teaching your children the value of work is to develop their character and their ability to earn money. Children who work with the proper attitude are more satisfied individuals. They grow up with more respect for the value of money and the effort required to earn it.

Income

It's important for children to have an income to learn the responsibility of handling money. The amount will vary according to such factors as the child's age, his ability to earn, and the financial circumstances

STARTLING STATS:

Children are exposed to electronic media an average of eight hours a day—watching TV, using a computer, listening to music, playing video games, and watching movies.

of the family. At first it is a new experience, and the child will make many mistakes. Do not hesitate to let the *law of consequences* run its course. You will be tempted to help little Johnny when he immediately spends all of his income unwisely. Neither he nor you will like the fact that he has to live the rest of the week without the other things he wants or needs. *But do not bail him out!* His mistakes will be his best teacher.

Parents should establish boundaries and offer advice on how to spend, but children must have freedom of choice within those boundaries. Excessive restrictions will only reduce opportunities to learn by experience. The first few dimes and quarters will make a lasting impression.

Every weekend I used to bicycle to the corner store with my son, Matthew, to buy him a pack of his favorite gum. Despite my advice, the entire pack would be consumed that day. When he started to receive an income, we decided that Matthew would have to buy his own gum. I will never forget the pained expression on his face as he came out of the store with his first purchase. "Daddy, this gum cost me all my money!" he blurted. That gum was rationed carefully and lasted more than a week.

A valuable lesson to teach children is to seek the Lord's provision through prayer. The Lord wants to demonstrate that He is actively involved in our lives. One way He does this is by answering prayers. We often rob children of this opportunity by buying or charging things without praying for God to supply them.

Budgeting

When children start to receive an income, teach them how to budget. Begin with a simple system consisting of three boxes, each labeled separately—*give*, *save*, and *spend*. Children distribute a portion of their income into each box. Thus a simple visual budget is established. Even a six-year-old can understand this method because when the spending box is empty, he can't buy anything else!

When children become teenagers, encourage them to use a budgeting software program. Teach them shopping skills, the ability to distinguish needs from wants, and the fine art of waiting on the Lord to provide. Warn them about the powerful influence of advertising and the danger of impulse spending.

Saving and Investing

Establish the habit of saving as soon as children receive an income. Begin by helping them open a savings account in their name. As they mature, expose them to various types of investments: stocks, bonds, real estate, etc. Teach children the benefits of compounding. If they grasp this concept and become faithful savers, they will enjoy financial health as adults.

Parents should demonstrate saving by saving for something that will directly benefit the children, such as a family vacation. Use a graph the children can fill in so they can visually chart the progress of the family's saving.

Debt

Teach children to avoid debt. One father I know loaned his son and daughter the money to buy bicycles. He drew up a repayment schedule that included the interest charged. After the children completed the long process of paying off the loans, the family celebrated with a "mortgage burning" ceremony at the beach. The father said that his children appreciated those bikes more than anything else they had and vowed to avoid debt in the future.

Giving

Early childhood is the best time to establish the habit of giving. It is helpful for children to give a portion of their gifts to a tangible need they can see. For example, when their gift helps to build the church under construction or buy food for a needy family they know, they can understand the impact of their gift.

> **HeyHoward@Crown.org**
>
> **QUESTION:** *Should I teach my children about the dangers of credit cards?*
> **ANSWER:** *Yes, the average college senior has $3,300 in credit card debt—and no job!*

PARENTS BECOME COACHES

As children leave home to marry or pursue their own careers, your role as a parent changes. Once they leave home, children no longer remain under your authority. The Bible says, *"A man will leave his father and mother and be united to his wife."*[5] Parents should assume the role of coach, mentor, and encourager.

Bev and I have thoroughly enjoyed this relationship with our children and their spouses. Parents *earn* this role by expressing their love and care to their children and their spouses in thoughtful and appropriate ways. Bev has been faithful to *"train the younger women to love their husbands and children, to be self-controlled and pure, to be busy at home, to be kind, and to be subject to their husbands."*[6] In return, our daughter and daughter-in-law call Bev almost every day asking for advice or just because they enjoy talking with her.

To Help or Not to Help—That Is the Question

When children become young adults, parents often are confused whether they should help them financially. Making these decisions requires discernment and prayer. If you can afford to, you may want to encourage them by giving to help with their needs. On the other hand, you don't want to give them money if it develops an entitlement mentality or interferes with God working in their lives through financial difficulties.

A basic rule of thumb: *Do not give adult children money if they are not making a serious effort to handle it God's way.* If they are working hard, spending carefully, and have a grateful attitude, then consider it.

When we've seen our children in need, more often than not we've sensed God was allowing this pressure to bring them and their spouses closer together and make them more reliant upon the Lord.

We are highly motivated to have them become completely debt free. So we've offered, as long as we are able, to match a portion of any prepayment they make on their home mortgages. They have made real progress toward getting their mortgages paid off and have appreciated this tangible expression of our love for them.

Grandparents Are Special

Grandparents have a unique opportunity to influence their grandchildren, both when they're young and as adults. It is important for grandparents to play a *complementary* role in which they affirm the objectives of the parents. Too often parents and grandparents have not agreed on how to train the youngest generation, and this can lead to bruised relationships and ineffective training. Together they should discuss how the grandparents can participate most effectively.

Passing our faith in Christ to the next generation can be compared to a relay race. Track coaches will tell you that relay races are often won or lost in the passing of the baton from one runner to another. Seldom is the baton dropped once it is firmly in a runner's grasp. If it is going to be dropped, it is in the exchange between the runners.

As parents we have the responsibility to pass the baton of practical biblical truths, including handling money, to our children. It's one of the most practical legacies you can leave your children and grandchildren. Make sure *your* life is characterized by generosity, spending within your means, saving consistently and staying out of debt. Modeling, communicating verbally, and offering real-life opportunities will form within your children the discipline and habits they need to faithfully handle money their entire lives.

As for the days of our life, they contain seventy years, or if due to strength, eighty years . . . for soon it is gone and we fly away. . . . So teach us to number our days that we may present to You [God] a heart of wisdom.

— MOSES

"The everyday choices I make regarding money will influence the very course of eternity."

— RANDY ALCORN

Author, Money, Possessions and Eternity

ETERNITY IS
FOREVER

On Monday, October 25, 1999, I checked out the news on the Internet as an unusual story unfolded. U.S. Air Force jets were following and trying unsuccessfully to communicate with the pilots of a private jet that had taken off from Orlando, Florida. News media were reporting the flight controllers had lost contact with the pilots and the plane was off course.

I didn't think much about it other than to pray for the safety of the plane's occupants. Thirty minutes later I received a phone call from a friend. "Howard, are you sitting down? I've got bad news. Robert Fraley and Van Ardan are on the airplane that just went down along with golfer Payne Stewart. There are no survivors."

Robert and Van were close friends of mine in their mid-forties. One of their most distinctive characteristics was the way they lived with an *eternal* perspective. Robert had painted these words of St. Augustine in his home workout area: "Take care of your body as though you will live forever; take care of your soul as if you will die tomorrow." Now they were in the eternal presence of their Creator.

AN ETERNAL PERSPECTIVE

When it comes to handling money, it is crucial to have an eternal perspective. Financial planners always encourage people to look down the road instead of simply focusing on today. "Don't think this year," they say. "Think thirty years from now."

We *should* think ahead, but far more than just thirty years—how about thirty *million* years! As someone once said, "He who provides for this life but does not consider eternity is wise for a moment but a fool forever." Jesus said it this way, *"What good is it for a man to gain the whole world, yet forfeit his soul?"*[1]

The Long and Short of It

Throughout the Bible we are told that life is brief. Moses asked God to help him number his days. *"As for the days of our life, they contain seventy years, or if due to strength, eighty years*[1] *. . . for soon it is gone. . . . So teach us to number our days, that we may present to You a heart of wisdom."*[2] I encourage you to number the days you might have left on earth. If I live as long as my father did, I have only about 7,300 days remaining. Being conscious of this has reminded me to invest my time and money on eternally important matters.

Life is short and eternity is long. What we do during this brief time on earth will matter forever.

When I served in the navy, the town in which I was stationed became my home and was the center of my attention. However, when I received orders discharging me in a few months, I became what was called a "short-timer." My focus shifted to my *real* hometown. In a similar way, when we realize that we are "short-timers" on earth and that we will soon be going to our *real* home, our focus shifts to things that are important in heaven. Author Matthew Henry said it this way, "It ought to be the business of every day to prepare for our last day."

Judgment

Because God loves you, He reveals in the Bible that there is a heaven and hell, that there is a coming judgment, and that He will grant eternal rewards for faithfulness. God wants the very best for you. Therefore, He wants to motivate you to handle money in such a way that you can enjoy a close relationship with Him now and receive the greatest possible rewards in heaven.

Although it may be uncomfortable to think about it, the Bible also reveals that everyone will be judged: *"They will have to give an account to him who is ready to judge the living and the dead."*[3] Those who do not know Christ will be sent to an indescribably dreadful place called hell. Those who know Christ will spend eternity with Him in heaven, an incredibly wonderful place.

All believers in Christ will give an account of their lives. *"We will all stand before God's judgment seat. . . . Each of us will give an account of himself to God."*[4] The result will be the gain or loss of eternal rewards. *"[Judgment] Day will bring it to light. . . . He will receive his reward . . . [or] he will suffer loss."*[5]

IMPACTING ETERNITY TODAY

People who do not know God often look at life as a brief interval that begins at birth and ends at death. They see no further than their own life span, so they often reason: *If this is all there is, why not spend money any way I please?*

Imagine a cable running through the room where you are now. It passes right in front of you, extending millions of light years to your right—all the way to the end of the universe. To your left, it extends all the way to the other end. Now imagine that the cable to your left represents eternity past, and the cable to your right, eternity future. If you were to place a small mark on the cable in front of you, it would represent your brief life on earth.

Because most people do not have an eternal perspective, they spend their money as if the *mark* immediately before them was all there is. They live in *mark* houses, drive *mark* cars, wear *mark* clothes, live *mark* lifestyles, and raise *mark* children.

However, we who know Christ have an entirely different view. We know that life is short, eternity is long, and what we do during our lifetime will matter forever.

Along with meeting our needs, the most important use of our money is to help other people. Jesus said, *"Use worldly wealth to gain friends for yourself, so that when it is gone, you will be welcomed into eternal dwellings.*[6] He is telling you to use money to meet others' needs and help them grow in their relationship with God. And when you die and money is no longer useful to you, the people you have influenced for Christ will welcome you into heaven.

What a phenomenal prospect! You can trade temporal possessions that you cannot keep anyway to gain eternal friendship and rewards that you cannot lose. Missionary martyr Jim Elliott said it this way, "He is no fool who gives what he cannot keep to gain what he cannot lose."

EVALUATE YOUR LIFE

God tells us that we live only once on earth; there is no such thing as reincarnation. *"It is appointed for men to die once and after this comes judgment."*[7] This life is the *only* opportunity you will have to influence people for eternity.

Those who dabble in developing photographs understand the effect of the "fixer." They immerse negatives in several different solutions, one of which is a developer. That developer solution parallels this life because as long as the photo stays in it, the photo is subject to change. But as soon as the photo is dropped into the fixer or "stop bath," it is permanently fixed. The photo is now done. So it will be when we enter eternity—our earthly lives will be fixed as they are, never to be revised.

Alfred Nobel was a Swedish chemist who made a fortune by inventing dynamite and other explosives used in weapons. When Nobel's brother died, a newspaper accidentally printed Alfred's obituary instead of his brother's. He was described as a man who became rich by enabling people to kill each other with powerful weapons. Shaken by this assessment, Nobel resolved to use his fortune to reward accomplishments that benefited humanity, originating what we now know as the Nobel Peace Prize.

Let us put ourselves in Nobel's place. Let us read our own obituary, not as written by people, but as it would be written from heaven's point of view. Then let us use the rest of our lives to edit that obituary into what we really want it to be.

When you are face-to-face with God and look back on your life, I pray that you will see that the things in which you invested your time, influence, and money are eternally significant. Please, don't squander your life on that which will not matter forever.[8]

YOU CAN KNOW GOD

I was twenty-eight years old when I started attending a weekly breakfast with several young businessmen. It wasn't long before I was impressed by their energy and business savvy. But more than that, I was attracted to the quality of their lives. I didn't know what they had, but whatever it was, I wanted it.

These men spoke openly of their faith in God. I grew up going to church but the religion I saw modeled for me as a youngster meant nothing to me as an adult. I had concluded it was only a fairy tale until a friend described how I could enter into a *personal* relationship with Jesus Christ. He explained several truths from the Bible I had never understood before.

God wants you to know Him and experience a meaningful life.

God desires a close relationship with each of us. The Bible teaches, *"God so loved the world that he gave his one and only Son, that whoever believes in him shall not perish but have eternal life."*[9] Jesus said, *"I came that they may have life, and have it abundantly."*[10]

Derek Redmond had dreamed all his life of winning the gold medal in the 400-meter race. He finally earned the opportunity to represent his homeland, Great Britain, during the 1992 Olympics in Barcelona, Spain. As the gun sounded for the semifinals, Derek knew that he had just started the race of his life.

Entering the backstretch at full speed, a torn hamstring shot searing pain up his right leg and sent him sprawling onto the track. Redmond instinctively struggled to get up. Then, in excruciating pain, he began hopping on one leg toward the finish line. He might not win, but he was determined to finish.

Suddenly, a large man came bounding from the stands. Pushing aside startled security guards, he crossed onto the track and threw his arms around

Derek. It was Jim Redmond, Derek's father.

"Son, you don't have to do this," he said.

"Yes, Dad, I do," Derek assured him.

"All right then, let's finish this together," said the older man. With head frequently buried in the father's shoulder, as Derek's body shuddered with pain, the young British runner, helped by his father, crossed the finish line. The watching crowd rose to its feet, weeping and cheering![11]

Derek Redmond did not win the gold medal that day. But he won something far more valuable. He walked away from the race with the memory of a father who not only cheered in the stands but also loved him too much to watch him suffer from a distance—a father who came down out of the stands and entered the race, staying with him every step of the way.

You, too, have a heavenly Father who watches your life with eyes of love and affection. He cared for you too deeply to stay in heaven, looking down on you, watching you struggle. Instead, He came down in the person of His Son, Jesus Christ, to carry you all the way home. And He is committed to staying in this race with you until you, too, cross safely past the finish line

We are separated from God.

God is holy—which simply means God is perfect, and He can't have a relationship with anyone who is not perfect. My friend asked if I'd ever sinned—done anything that would disqualify me from perfection. "Many times," I admitted. He explained that every person has sinned, and its consequence is separation from God. *"All have sinned and fall short of the glory of God."*[12]

This following diagram illustrates our separation from God:

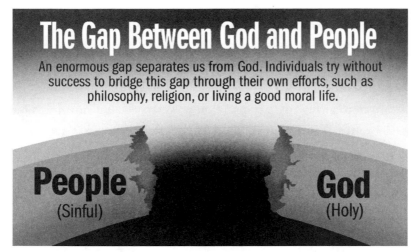

An enormous gap separates us from God. Individuals try without success to bridge this gap through their own efforts. Nothing—not education, money, philosophy, or living a good life—can bridge the gap between God and us.

God's only provision to bridge this gap is Jesus Christ.

Jesus Christ died on the cross to bridge the gap between God and us. Jesus said, *'I am the way and the truth and the life. No one comes to the Father except through me.'* "[13]

This diagram illustrates our union with God through Jesus Christ:

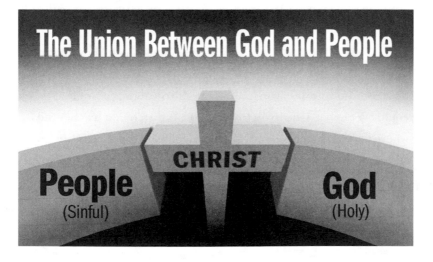

This relationship is a gift from God.

My friend explained that by an act of faith I could receive the free gift of a relationship with God. The transaction appeared unfair. I had learned in business that any time two people were convinced they were getting more than they were giving up, a transaction was assured. But now I was being offered a relationship with God, and it was a free gift! *"For it is by grace you have been saved, through faith—and this is not from yourselves, it is the gift of God—not by works, so that no one can boast."*[14]

I had only to ask Jesus Christ to come into my life to be my Savior and Lord. So I did! As my friends will tell you, I am a very practical person—if something doesn't work, I stop doing it quickly. I can tell you from more than thirty years of experience that a relationship with the living God works. And it is available to you through Jesus Christ. Nothing in life compares with the privilege of knowing Christ personally. We can experience true peace, joy, and hope when we know Him. It's the only way you can enjoy *true financial freedom.*

If you want to know God and are not certain whether you have this relationship, I encourage you to receive Jesus Christ right now. Pray a prayer similar to the one I prayed: "God, I need You. I'm sorry for my sin. I invite Jesus to come into my life as my Savior and Lord and to make me the person You want me to be. Thank You for forgiving my sins and giving me the gift of eternal life."

You might go all the way on your journey and reach Destination 7, but without a relationship with Christ, it won't have any lasting value. If you asked Christ into your life, you have made the most important decision anyone could ever make. I urge you to find a local church that teaches the Bible, one where you can begin to learn what it means to follow Jesus Christ.

Roadside Assistance—Online!

To learn more about growing in a relationship with Jesus Christ, visit Crown MoneyMap.org.

The greatest use of life is to spend it for something that will outlast it.

—WILLIAM JAMES

Make all you can, save all you can, give all you can.

—JOHN WESLEY

CHAPTER 22

DESTINATION 7:
TRUE FINANCIAL
FREEDOM

Once again it was time to replace our car. We drove twenty
miles to do business with a dealership that had a great reputation for honesty. Bev and I smiled at each other when we saw the sign—*Mitchell Autos.*
After trading for a newer model, we sat in Matt's office and reminisced.[1]

"Matt, you and Jennifer have come a long way since the first time we
bought a car from you," Bev marveled.

"We are so grateful," Matt said. "We don't have one penny of debt and
our kids' education and our retirement are funded. And on top of that, the
car business is thriving.

"Who could have guessed that when I started as Mr. Johnson's management trainee, he would end up selling me one of his dealerships for such a
reasonable price? Jennifer and I are convinced this is what the Lord wants
me to do for the rest of my life. We want to use this business to help fund
what God is doing around the world."

"Matt, what are the first words you want to hear from the Lord when
you enter heaven?" I asked.

"Well done, good and faithful servant!" [2] Matt responded without hesitation.

"That's what every person who knows Christ as Savior should want to hear," I said, "the same words Jesus used in a parable praising a servant for handling money well." [3]

> *"There is no earthly requirement that I myself personally need. God has blessed me with an abundance of everything that wealth can furnish for my own necessities, and therefore, I am not hungry after more earthly goods for myself, but I am beyond measure greedy on behalf of God's cause."*
>
> CHARLES H. SPURGEON,
> *speaking at an orphanage*
> *at Stockwell, England*

CONGRATULATIONS . . . AND A HEADS UP

Congratulations on reaching Destination 7— *true financial freedom.* I hope you have celebrated God's goodness every step of the way. Your journey has probably been a long one, requiring a lot of perseverance, patience, and effort. That's how it was for Bev and me. Those who reach *true financial freedom* will encounter three potential dangers that can jeopardize their finishing well and hearing the words, "Well done."

1. The Danger of Trusting in Things

It's human nature to cling to the Lord when it is clear that we need Him. However, once we become financially free, it is human nature to take God for granted.

A father was carrying his two-year-old son as he waded in a lake. Even though the water was deep enough to drown him, the son was unconcerned as long as the safety of the beach was nearby. But the farther they moved away from shore, the tighter the child held on.

Like the child, we are always completely dependent upon the Lord to provide, but we often don't recognize our need when we are "close to shore," enjoying what *seems* to be financial security. This is a tremendous struggle because we tend to trust in the seen rather than in the unseen. It is easy to look to our assets to meet our needs instead of the invisible, living God. Our possessions can become our god.

God recognized this danger and warned those who are financially free,

"Instruct those who are rich [financially free] *in this present world not . . . to fix their hope on the uncertainty of riches, but on God, who richly supplies us with all things to enjoy."*[4] The only way you can overcome this challenge is to nurture your relationship with Christ by regularly reading the Bible and spending time with him in prayer, reminding yourself that He is the Owner and Provider.

> Money will buy:
> A bed but not sleep;
> Books but not common sense;
> Food but not an appetite;
> A house but not a home;
> Medicine but not health;
> A crucifix but not a Savior.
>
> Anonymous

2. The Danger of Not Giving Generously

God wants those who are financially free to be generous for their *own* bene-fit. The Bible says, *"Instruct those who are rich* [financially free] *. . . to be generous and ready to share, storing up for themselves the treasure of a good foundation for the future, so that they may take hold of that which is life indeed."*[5] According to this passage, two remarkable benefits flow to financially free people who are generous.

- Treasures that they will enjoy throughout all eternity
- The blessing of taking *"hold of that which is life indeed"* during their time on earth

Many people believe that following God will be a boring experience—complete with long faces and endless lists of things they cannot do. Nothing could be further from the truth. The Creator of the universe intends us to live vibrant, fulfilling lives. Nothing on this planet comes close to knowing Christ and taking *"hold of that which is life indeed."*[6] And one of the keys to experiencing this quality of life is to give generously.

3. The Danger of Retirement

The goal of retirement is deeply ingrained in our culture. Many financially free people retire to pursue a life dedicated to leisure. The Bible gives no examples of people retiring, and only one reference relates to the subject: an instruction that applied exclusively to Old Testament workers at the place God's people were to worship.[7]

People who are physically and mentally capable should not retire and become unproductive. In a parable, Jesus strongly rebukes the notion of a life of leisure for the financially free: *"I'll say to myself, 'You have plenty of good things laid up for many years. Take life easy; eat, drink and be merry.' But God said to him, 'You fool!'"*[8] A proper amount of leisure is important and pleasing to God. Recreational sports and hobbies are wonderful diversions but become unhealthy as full-time activities or the focus of life.

In the Bible, we have the sense that the type or intensity of work may change as we grow older. There is a shifting of the gears to a less demanding pace. During this season of life we can benefit others by actively using the experiences and wisdom we have gained over a lifetime.

HeyHoward@Crown.org

QUESTION: *Is it okay with God for me to retire from my job?*
ANSWER: *Yes, you may retire from your job. However, as long as you are physically able, you should be actively involved in service to God.*

This is important to understand. If you continue in your job after becoming financially free, become *extraordinarily* generous. Since you no longer need your income to live on, you can give much of it away. On the other hand, if you retire from your job, *never* retire from actively serving the Lord. If you sense God wants you to retire or cut back on your work, volunteer more time to serve in your church or in a ministry to others.

That is what Bev and I sensed the Lord wanted for us. I am thankful to have been a full-time volunteer at Crown Financial Ministries since 1985. I've never worked harder or enjoyed it more. He may have something similar for you. *True financial freedom* means you give more of your income and time for eternally significant purposes.

FOR SUCH A TIME AS THIS!

I have wrestled with whether to share this with you because it is risky. Some of you may misunderstand and think I'm too flaky to be believable. However, I'm willing to assume the risk for the sake of motivating the rest of you.

In 1977, I was alone writing my first book. Suddenly, God overcame me and clearly communicated two things. First, that during my lifetime, America would experience a very difficult time financially. And second, He conveyed through a verse in the Bible, *"You have been called . . . for such a time as this."*[9] He wanted me to help others on their journey to true financial freedom.

This is the only time God has ever communicated with me in such a powerful and unmistakable way, and it fueled my passion for helping others. He did not divulge the catalyst for this financial difficulty nor when it will occur. My sense is that it is probably years in the future. However, the financial storm is gathering on the horizon.

The Bible warns us that there are consequences when we disobey God. One of them is *"The alien . . . will rise above you higher and higher, but you will sink lower and lower. He will lend to you, but you will not lend to him."*[10] Look at the

graph and see the staggering growth of our national debt to foreigners. In a little over twenty years, the United States has gone from *owning* about seven percent to *owing* 40 percent. This represents a gigantic shift of trillions of dollars!

You now know God's way of handling money, but knowing is only half the answer. You must also do it. Jesus said, *"Everyone who hears these words of mine and **puts them into practice** is like a wise man who built his house upon the rock. The rain came down, the streams rose, and the winds blew and beat against that house; yet it did not fall, because it had its foundation on the rock."*[11]

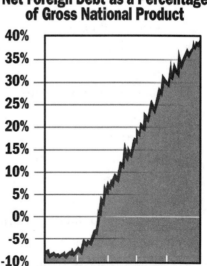

Net Foreign Debt as a Percentage of Gross National Product

SOURCE: Ralph Dudera, Spectrum Financial

The economic rain and floods are gathering against this nation's financial house. If you have built your house on the rock-solid principles found in the Bible, your financial house will not fall. So I plead with you to seize this opportunity! Give generously, save, and get out of debt. Become a faithful steward. Make progress on your journey to true financial freedom.

TEACH OTHERS

One of the best ways for you to make progress on your financial journey is to *teach* others. I've taught more than fifty Crown small group studies. The people in these groups have made huge financial progress, but the person who benefited most was me.

You don't have to wait until you have reached Destination 7 before you teach; you don't even have to reach Destination 1. You only need to be willing to make progress. Crown has tens of thousands of volunteers helping to teach others. So take others through this book, or lead a Crown ten-week small group study, or become a Money Map coach. One of the best ways to demonstrate your love for your family and friends is to get your financial house in order and encourage them to do the same.

FINISH WELL

According to Dr. Howard Hendricks, of the 2,930 individuals mentioned in the Bible, we know significant details of only 100. Of those 100, only about one-third finished well. Of the two-thirds that did not finish well, most failed in the second half of their lives. Finishing well for those who are financially free is especially challenging because of the options money can buy. Many of these can distract us from serving Christ.

In your journey with God, it's not how you start that matters, it's how you finish. What will you do to become the one in three who reaches the finish line still serving Christ? You will need to make wise choices to have a strong finishing kick when you hit the tape at age sixty-five, eighty-five, or whatever age God calls you home.

While writing this book, I have prayed for you. I have prayed that every reader would understand God's way of handling money, and that you would make significant progress in your financial journey. And remember, even if you don't reach Destination 7, with God's help you can move forward. You can enjoy more financial health and stability and you can finish well.

STARTLING STATS:

Of the 100 individuals the Bible mentions with significant detail, two-thirds did not finish well. Most failed in the second half of their lives.

Finishing well was a priority for the apostle Paul. He said, *"I consider my life worth nothing to me, if only I may finish the race and complete the task the Lord Jesus has given me."* [12] And he did it: *"I have fought the good fight, I have finished the race, I have kept the faith.* [13] Jesus finished well. He said, *"I have brought you* [God the Father] *glory on earth by completing the work you gave me to do."* [14]

For three years, I watched Crown's cofounder, Larry Burkett, battle life-threatening cancer and heart disease. Until his last breath, Larry never stopped working to complete the task that God had given him.

More than anything, I pray that you will be faithful in handling money and investing your time in that which is eternally significant. May you finish well and hear those priceless words, *"Well done, good and faithful [servant] . . . Enter into the joy of your master."* [15]

"The greatest use of life is to spend it for something that will outlast it."

WILLIAM JAMES

6 MAKING PROGRESS ON THE JOURNEY

I often told my parents, who founded our wholesale electrical supply business, "I have no intentions of ever getting out of debt. It'd be almost un-American to get rid of it." I had amassed *$5 million* of business debt and significant personal debt as well.

Sherra and I joined a Crown small group study, and our view completely changed. When we saw how clearly the Bible discourages debt, we decided to try to eliminate our millions of dollars of debt. We knew we couldn't begin to do it without God's help. So we prayed, and we used every extra penny to reduce our mountain of debt.

Several months later, we sold some inherited agricultural property and paid off our home. I can remember leaving the bank after paying it off. All I could think about was what Jesus said, *"You will know the truth, and the truth will set you free."*[16] I felt so free!

We continued making steady progress to reduce the business debt, but it was so slow it looked like it would take us a lifetime. Then, three years later, out of the blue a large company offered to buy our business. We decided to sell, become debt free, and reach true financial freedom.

I never realized how much stress I was under. My migraine headaches all but disappeared. I was free to serve Christ without the need for a salary. I became a trained counselor serving at my church for five years as a volunteer. During that time, God used me to introduce about five hundred people to Jesus Christ as their Savior. I traded $5 million of debt for five hundred people who will be in heaven forever!

One interesting footnote: Shortly after selling, a deep recession caused business losses that would have forced us into bankruptcy had we not sold. We couldn't have sold if we hadn't been making progress paying down our debt.

—GERALD AND SHERRA JONES, *Orlando, Florida*

DISCUSSION QUESTIONS

1. How well were you prepared to handle money when you left home as a young person? Describe how you will train children to manage money God's way.

2. Estimate the number of days you have left on earth. How does this impact your thinking? What actions will you take to ensure you finish your life well from God's perspective?

3. What do you plan on doing in your retirement that is eternally significant? How will you prepare for it?

4. What was the most beneficial part of studying this book for you?

5. With whom could you share the life-changing message of this book? Ask God to bring someone to your mind. What will you do to continue to learn more about God's way of handling money? How will you teach this to others?

TOOLS FOR YOUR JOURNEY

Learning about eternity

Money, Possessions and Eternity, Randy Alcorn (Wheaton, Ill.: Tyndale, 1989).

Helping the financially free grow

Special Edition small group study, Crown Financial Ministries.

APPENDIX

INSURANCE

There are many types of insurance: life, health, disability, homeowners, and liability for starters. Once you settle on the types of insurance you need, then determine how much you can afford. At this time, you may not be able to purchase all the insurance you need. If you are in this situation, prioritize which you should purchase first.

Because insurance can be complex, I will address only the basics in this appendix. To learn more, visit CrownMoneyMap.org. And please, get advice from knowledgeable professionals when making insurance decisions.

LIFE INSURANCE

The purpose of life insurance is to provide for loved ones when a bread winner dies. Completing the Life Insurance Worksheet at the end of this appendix will give you a rough idea of how much life insurance to carry.

Although there are many variations, there are three basic types of life insurance: whole life, universal life, and term. Whole life and universal life combine death coverage with a savings program. Because of the savings component, they are more expensive than term. Term life insurance has no saving program and offers much more coverage for the same premium. If you choose term, I recommend purchasing ten- to twenty-year *level* term that is guaranteed renewable. With these, the premium remains the same for ten or twenty years regardless of your health.

HEALTH INSURANCE

With the skyrocketing cost of health care, health insurance is a *super high* priority. Without it, you are one major illness away from major financial problems. The National Bankruptcy Commission discovered that about 50 percent of bankruptcies stem from overwhelming medical bills. If your employer does not provide health insurance, shop for the best deal because health insurance is expensive.

HOMEOWNER'S INSURANCE

Homeowner's insurance covers the majority of risks to your home and contents. It also covers some personal liability in the event someone is injured on your property. It is important to know the difference between actual cash value insurance and guaranteed replacement value.

Actual cash value refers to the *depreciated* value of items. A policy that pays on this basis might allow $50 for a couch that is several years old even though it might cost you ten times as much to replace it with a new one. *Guaranteed replacement value* means that your home and contents are covered at 100 percent of the cost to replace them with new items. This type of homeowner's insurance is more expensive but well worth it.

If you rent, *renter's insurance* covers your furniture and personal property and also provides liability coverage if someone is injured.

DISABILITY INSURANCE

Carrying disability insurance is also a high priority. The most economical way to get it is through your employer, either as a provided benefit or as an addition to your health insurance coverage. This is usually a *group* plan that pays benefits on a percentage of your wage.

Since each policy has its own definition of disability, read it carefully. The best definition requires the inability to perform the main duties of "*your* occupation" before coverage kicks in. The definition "*any* occupation" means that benefits are not paid unless you are unable to perform *any* job.

As with most kinds of insurance, you have choices that will affect its cost. For instance, it is common to have a waiting period of sixty days from the time of the disability until benefits begin, but you can lower your premium for accepting a longer waiting period. Another choice involves how long benefits will continue. Policies pay for a defined time—anywhere from one year up to age sixty-five. The longer a policy is required to pay, the more expensive it will be. You may also have a choice regarding the percentage of your regular income the policy will pay.

AUTOMOBILE INSURANCE

Full coverage on a car includes all basic coverage: bodily injury, liability, property damage, medical, uninsured motorists, collisions, and comprehensive. If you have a newer car or a car loan, carry *full coverage*. The lower the cash value of your car, the less benefit there is for having full coverage. Discuss the options with your agent to determine what is best for you.

Most states require you to carry *liability insurance* on your car to cover the other person's costs if there is an accident. Even if your state does not require it, carry it because your risk is huge, and the cost is relatively small. If you don't, one accident can wipe out your finances.

LIABILITY INSURANCE

An *umbrella liability* policy is an inexpensive way to get extra liability coverage not provided by your other policies. Generally, it's best to buy an umbrella policy from the same company that provides your homeowner's insurance.

LIFE INSURANCE WORKSHEET

Estimate family's annual income needs if
breadwinner dies   _____

Subtract other income available
(Social Security, investments, retirement,
surviving spouse's income, etc.)   _____

Equals Net Annual Income needed   _____

Multiply Net Annual Income needed by 12.5   _____

Add lump sum needs
    Debts   _____
    Education   _____
    Other   _____
Total lump sum needs   _____

Equals life insurance needed   _____

Explanations

To estimate the amount of insurance you should carry, multiply the "Net Annual Income" needed by 12.5. This assumes the survivors will earn an 8 percent return, after taxes, on the insurance proceeds. For example, if "Net Annual Income" of $10,000 is needed to support the survivors: *Multiply* $10,000 by 12.5. This *equals* $125,000 in life insurance coverage. (Multiply the net annual income by at least 15 if you think you will earn less than 8 percent.)

Lump Sum Requirements

In addition to providing regular income, insurance can provide "lump sums" for debt repayment or other purposes. Identify those needs and add them to the amount of insurance needed for income. Once you have calculated your life insurance needs, deduct the amount of your present coverage to determine whether you need additional life insurance.

NOTES

Since the verse divisions and numbers were not included in the Bible until 1560 A.D., I haven't always quoted the *entire* verse, but rather focused on the phrase that was appropriate. My model for this is Jesus and how He and the apostles quoted the Old Testament. They often just quoted a phrase to make a point.

Chapter 1: The Challenge
1. Stephen Roach, Morgan Stanley economist, November 1, 2004.

Chapter 2: The Solution
1. Proverbs 24:3–4 (TLB, emphasis mine.)
2. Luke 1:37.
3. Philippians 3:13–14.
4. Isaiah 55:8.

Chapter 3: Your Money Map
1. Proverbs 21:5 (TLB).

Chapter 4: Who's the Real Owner?
1. Luke16:11. The word faithful from the NASB is substituted for trustworthy from the NIV to clarify the meaning.

2. Matthew 6:24.
3. Psalm 24:1.
4. Leviticus 25:23.
5. Haggai 2:8.
6. Psalm 50:10–12.
7. Psalm 135:6.
8. 1 Chronicles 29:11 (TLB).
9. Romans 8:28 (NASB).
10. Genesis 45:5, 8; 50:20.
11. Romans 5:3–4.
12. Hebrews 12: 6, 10.
13. Matthew 6:33.
14. Exodus 16:35.
15. Matthew 14:17.
16. Isaiah 51:13.
17. Isaiah 40:26 (NASB).
18. Psalm 139:3–4, 16.

19. Matthew 10:30.
20. Jeremiah 32:17.

Chapter 5: We Are Managers

1. 1 Corinthians 4:2 (NASB). The word faithful from the NIV is substituted for trustworthy from the NASB to clarify the meaning.
2. Matthew 25:14–15.
3. Matthew 25:21.
4. Hosea 4:6.
5. Luke 16:10 (NASB).
6. Zechariah 4:10 (NLT).
7. David McConaughy, *Money the Acid Test* (Old Tappan: NJ: Revell, 1919), xx.
8. Matthew 11:28, 30.

Chapter 6: Giving

1. John 3:16.
2. 1 John 4:8.
3. 1 Corinthians 13:3 (NASB).
4. Matthew 23:23 (TLB).
5. Acts 20:35 (NASB).
6. Matthew 6:21.
7. Matthew 6:20.
8. Philippians 4:17.
9. Proverbs 11:24–25.
10. 2 Corinthians 9:6.
11. Malachi 3:8.
12. Galatians 6:6 (NASB).
13. Galatians 2:10.
14. Matthew 25:35–40, emphasis mine.

Chapter 7: Honesty

1. Romans 13:9–10 (TLB).
2. Judges 17:6 (NASB).
3. Proverbs 13:11 (NASB).
4. Proverbs 20:23 (TLB).
5. Proverbs 6:16–17.
6. Exodus 20:15.
7. John 14:6.
8. 1 Peter 1:15–16 (NASB).
9. John 8:44.

10. Matthew 22:37 (NASB).
11. Proverbs 3:32 (NASB).
12. Romans 13:9-10 (TLB).
13. Proverbs 4:24–26 (NASB).
14. Luke 16:10.
15. Genesis 14:22–23 (NASB).
16. Leviticus 6:4–5 (NASB).
17. Luke 19:8 (NASB).
18. Exodus 23:8 (NASB).
19. Luke 20:22–25.
20. Romans 13:1, 6–7.

Chapter 8: It's Time to Party!

1. Deuteronomy 16:13–15.
2. John 15:5.

Chapter 9: What on Earth Am I Here For?

1. Matthew 19:26.
2. Acts 13:36, emphasis mine.
3. Jeremiah 1:5.
4. Ephesians 2:10.
5. Ephesians 2:10 (AMP).
6. Romans 12:6 (TLB).
7. Hebrews 4:12.
8. 2 Corinthians 1:3–4 (TLB).

Chapter 10: Making the Most Out of Your Job

1. Genesis 2:15.
2. Exodus 34:21 (NASB).
3. 2 Thessalonians 3:10 (NASB).
4. Exodus 36:1, emphasis mine.
5. Psalm 75:6-7 (TLB).
6. Genesis 39:2–3.
7. Ecclesiastes 9:10.
8. Proverbs 12:27 (NASB).
9. Proverbs 18:9 (NASB).
10. Exodus 34:21 (NASB).
11. Colossians 3:23-24 (NASB).
12. Developed by the University of Georgia.
13. 1 Peter 2:18.

Chapter 11: Destination 1: Saving for Emergencies

1. Proverbs 21:20 (TLB).
2. Proverbs 30:24–25.
3. Genesis 41:29.
4. Genesis 41:30.
5. Philippians 4:11–13.
6. 1 Corinthians 3:16–17.
7. Proverbs 21:20 (TLB).
8. Proverbs 22:7.
9. Philippians 4:6 emphasis mine.
10. Mark 3:25.

Chapter 12: Destination 1: Your Spending Plan

1. Genesis 2:24 (NASB).

Chapter 14: Destination 3: Consumer Debt Paid Off

1. Psalm 37:21.
2. Proverbs 17:18 (NLT).

Chapter 15: Destination 4: Saving for Major Purchases

1. Greg Toppo, "College graduates see their debt burden increase," *USA Today*, 28 March 2005.
2. Proverbs 22:7.

Chapter 16: Destination 4: Saving to Start Your Own Business

1. Ephesians 3:20 (TLB).
2. *USA Today*, 20 April 2005, "Your Money" section.
3. Proverbs 24:27 (TLB).
4. Psalm 32:8.
5. Isaiah 9:6.
6. See Porter B. Williamson, *Patton's Principles: For Managers Who Really Mean It* (New York: Touchstone, 1975).
7. 2 Corinthians 6:14–15 (NASB).

Chapter 17: Destination 5: Buying Your Home and Paying It Off

1. Proverbs 21:5 (TLB).

Chapter 18: Destination 5: Investing

1. Luke 12:16–21, 34, emphasis mine.
2. 1 Timothy 6:9.
3. 1 Timothy 6:10.
4. Genesis 24:35;1 Chronicles 29:28.
5. Proverbs 21:5 (TLB).
6. Proverbs 19:20.
7. Genesis 2:18.
8. Ecclesiastes 11:2 (NASB).
9. Psalm 37:21 (NASB).
10. Ecclesiastes 5:13–15 (TLB).
11. John and Sylvia Ronsvalle, *The State of Church Giving* (Champaign, IL: Empty Tomb).

Chapter 19: Destination 6: Planning Your Estate

1. 2 Kings 20:1.
2. 1 Timothy 6:7.
3. Proverbs 13:22 (NASB).
4. Proverbs 20:21 (NASB).
5. Galatians 4:1–2.
6. Luke 12:13, 15.
7. I want to thank Ron Blue for providing material for this chapter from his outstanding book *Splitting Heirs* (Chicago: Moody, 2004).

Chapter 20: This Is a Family Trip!

1. Proverbs 22:6 (NASB).
2. Luke 16:10 (NASB).
3. 1 Corinthians 11:1 (NASB).
4. Deuteronomy 6:6–7 (NASB).
5. Genesis 2:24.
6. Titus 2:4–5.

Chapter 21: Eternity Is Forever

1. Mark 8:36.
2. Psalm 90:10, 12 (NASB).
3. 1 Peter 4:5.
4. Romans 14:10–12.
5. 1 Corinthians 3:13–15.
6. Luke 16:9.
7. Hebrews 9:27 (NASB).
8. I thank Randy Alcorn for providing material for much of this chapter from his excellent book *Money, Possessions and Eternity* (Wheaton, IL: Tyndale, 1989). Used by permission.
9. John 3:16.
10. John 10:10 (NASB).
11. Claire Cloninger, *Dear Abba*, (Dallas: Word 1997), 14–15.
12. Romans 3:23.
13. John 14:6.
14. Ephesians 2:8–9.

Chapter 22: Destination 7: True Financial Freedom

1. Matt and Jennifer Mitchell are a fictitious couple. They represent people whom Crown Financial Ministries has assisted over the years.
2. Matthew 25:21.
3. Matthew 25:14–30.
4. 1 Timothy 6:17 (NASB).
5. 1 Timothy 6:17–19 (NASB).
6. 1 Timothy 6:17–19.
7. Numbers 8:24–26.
8. Luke 12:19–20.
9. Esther 4:14.
10. Deuteronomy 28:43–44.
11. Matthew 7:24–27, emphasis mine.
12. Acts 20:24.
13. 2 Timothy 4:7.
14. John 17:4.
15. Matthew 25:21 (NASB).
16. John 8:32.

Choose Your Budgeting Solution!

Choose your preferred spending plan, and get started on the journey to true financial freedom! We have a budget that will be perfect for you.

ISBN# 1-56427-049-1

PC-Based Software

Crown Money Map Financial Software

- Track income and expenses, investments, set up reminders, and more.
- It teaches you how to budget based on God's way of handling money.
- Compatible with Windows, Mac, and Linux platforms
- Free 30-day trial available online

Web-Based Software

Crown Personal Mvelopes

- Available online anytime, anywhere
- Secure access and convenient bill-paying capability
- Low monthly subscription
- Free 30-day trial and online tutorial available

ISBN# 0-8027-1478-8

Paper

Family Financial Workbook

- Create a paper budgeting system and customize it to fit your needs.
- Provides all of the forms you need to start and maintain a budget.
- Follow the recommended spending plan to gain financial freedom.

ISBN# 1-56427-059-9

Cash Spending

Cash Organizer

- Ideal for people who spend or pay bills with cash
- Physically separates your money in category spending envelopes
- When there's no money left in a category, you're finished spending!

For more information, contact your local Christian Retailer or go to CrownMoneyMap.org.

*Career*DIRECT

Complete Guidance System

You have unlimited potential to be more, do more, and maximize your God-given talents and abilities. You want more than a career—you want a true calling for your life.

The *Career Direct® Complete Guidance System* is an online personal growth resource designed to maximize your effectiveness in life and work. It is one of the only time-tested, revolutionary assessments that profiles four areas: **Personality, Interests, Skills, and Values,** to help you grow and make the best choice in your life and career.

Developed over a 10-year period, more than 120,000 people of all ages have trusted *Career Direct* to help them find their calling. Just think, in about an hour, you will receive a comprehensive, easy-to-read personalized report, and additional online resources will help you create an action plan to immediately start you on a path to growth and fulfillment. **Career Direct is ready to assist you!**

Learn More...and Stay
Connected
on Your Journey

There are several ways for you to learn more of God's practical financial advice and connect with others who will encourage you on your journey. To make faster progress and have fun doing it, choose one of these popular options and get connected.

ONLINE
The *Crown Money Map* support Web site has a wealth of resources, encouraging stories and videos, free online journal, and more to keep you connected. It's a world that will help you succeed!

LIVE SEMINAR
Journey to True Financial Freedom is the perfect one-day seminar to learn how to apply God's way of handling your money.
Visit *CrownMoneyMap.org* to find a seminar in your area taught by a trained Crown seminar instructor.

VIDEO WORKSHOP
Video workshops are great for individual or group study in homes, churches, or businesses. Available in a variety of financial topics that are convieniently taught in six lessons, you will gain a deeper understanding about God's financial principles.

SMALL GROUP STUDY
This is the most powerful study Crown offers. In only ten weeks, this small-group study will change your life and improve your finances. The average graduate pays off about $20,000 of debt and increases their savings $10,000—within just three years of finishing the study. Close relationships are formed among those in the group. The study is often offered through local churches.

For more information, go to CrownMoneyMap.org!